John Monteath

Dunblane Traditions

Being a Series of warlike and legendary Narratives, biographical Sketches

of eccentric Characters, &c.

John Monteath

Dunblane Traditions
Being a Series of warlike and legendary Narratives, biographical Sketches of eccentric Characters, &c.

ISBN/EAN: 9783337071806

Printed in Europe, USA, Canada, Australia, Japan

Cover: Foto ©ninafisch / pixelio.de

More available books at **www.hansebooks.com**

DUNBLANE TRADITIONS;

BEING A SERIES OF

WARLIKE AND LEGENDARY NARRATIVES,

BIOGRAPHICAL SKETCHES OF ECCENTRIC

CHARACTERS, &c.

COMPILED FROM ANECDOTES GLEANED FROM THE TALES OF OLD
PEOPLE IN DUNBLANE AND VICINITY.

TO WHICH IS ADDED

AN APPENDIX

OF

ORIGINAL POEMS AND SONGS,

COLLECTED BY

JOHN MONTEATH.

STIRLING:
PRINTED BY E. JOHNSTONE, BOOKSELLER.
MDCCCXXXV.

GLASGOW:
REPRINTED BY JOHN MILLER, 116 RENFIELD ST.
1887.

CONTENTS.

I.
WARLIKE TALES AND ANECDOTES.

	PAGE.
I. Battle Memorials of Wallace in Sheriff-muir,	5
II. The Auld Laird o' Balhaldie,	9
III. The MacGregors and "The Shirra-Moor,"	14
IV. Anecdotes of the Battle of Sheriff-muir,	18
V. Dunblane Anecdotes of "The Forty-Five"—	
No. 1.—The Highland Army,	20
2.—The Royal Army,	24
VI. Auld Calzie,	34
VII. Young Rob Roy,	39
VIII. Anecdotes of "The Forty-Five"—	
No. 1.—Battle of Falkirk,	42
2.—Battle of Gladsmuir,	43
3.—Duke William and a Highlander,	44

II.
LEGENDARY TALES.

I. The Black Knight of Kilbryde,	47
II. The Witches o' Logie,	50
III. Doctor Ure,	53
IV. The Laird o' Argaty,	58
V. The Warlock o' Dunblane,	61
VI. Fair Queen Helen,	65

III.
BIOGRAPHICAL SKETCHES.

I. Bessy Stein,	69
II. Sandy Robieson.	75
III. Henry Reid,	79
IV. The Muckle Wife o' Bithergirse,	83
V. Auld Willie o' the Back-hills,	93
VI. Maggy o' the Bog,	96
VII. The Black Laird,	98

IV.

ORIGINAL POETRY.

	PAGE.
Jacobitical Song,	107
Dunblane Wells,	109
Verses on Sheriff-muir,	111
Stanza,	112
The Wives o' Dunblane,	113
The Bracs o' Cauldhame,	114
Donal o' Dunblane,	116
To the Willow,	118
Moony Madness,	119
Woman,	121
Wispy,	121
Fragments,	122
The Dunblane Wife's Lilt,	123

V.

Subscribers to the First Edition of Monteath's Dunblane Traditions, ... 125 to 135

Warlike Tales and Anecdotes.

I.

BATTLE MEMORIALS OF WALLACE IN SHERIFF-MUIR.

ABOUT two miles south-west of the village of Blackford, on the Sheriff-muir road, and near to the farm-house of Easter-Biggs, is an arch of stones, seven in number, called the "Seven Stanes," varying from perhaps a ton to two tons each. One of these is of a round prismatical shape, and stands in an erect position. Beside these lies a large bullet of stone, called "Wallace's Puttin' Stane," and he is accounted a strong man who can *lift* it in his arms to the top of the standing one, which is about four feet high,—and a *very* strong man who is able to toss it over without coming in contact with the upright one. At one time few were to be found of such muscular strength as to accomplish this—not so much from the actual weight of the stone itself, as from the difficulty of retaining hold of it, it being very smooth and circular. This difficulty, however, was obviated about seventy years ago, by the barbarous hand of a mason, to enable himself to perform the feat, since which time a person of ordinary strength can easily lift it. Some three miles farther south, by the same road, and near to Cauldhame farm, on a pretty extensive heathy dale of Balhaldie Muir, about a mile to the east of the scene of action in 1715, are five stones placed in a line, due east and west. Two of these are large, not less than fifteen or twenty tons each, and one of them still stands upright. They are known by the appellation of "The Stan'in' Stanes;" from which it may be inferred that, in former times, they had been all standing upright. About two miles farther on, to the west of the same line of road to Stirling, near to the mansion-house of Pendreigh, and upon a rising ground, now covered with a thriving plantation, is another remarkable stone standing upon end; and at a place called Whiteheadston, two or three miles north of Dunblane, is another large Upright-Stone,* similar to the "Stan'in' Stane," and that on the Black-hill of Pendreigh.

It now remains for us to inquire what ancient oral

---

* It was at this stone—"the Muckle Stane o' Whitestoun,"—that "the first Whig blood was drawn," in 1715, on the morning of that day when a thousand claymores were dyed red with human blood on the heights of Sheriff-muir. Our oralists relate that, according to the superstitious code of their belief, it was deemed by some individuals of the Clans, indispensable to ensure their success in battle, that the blood of an enemy should be shed previous to the commencement of the onset. No stray "red-coat" having fallen into their clutches, it was immediately resolved that they should secretly select a Whig victim from the little hamlet of Whiteheadston, and there, "in cauld bluid," sacrifice him while the lines were forming to ascend the muir. A person of the name of Dawson was seized for this purpose, but he, it is said, guessing what was intended, counterfeited so well, that his intending murderers were persuaded he could be no Whig, but a friend of *the* King—"King Hamish." Another man, however, was less fortunate, being transfixed with broad-swords at "the Muckle Stane," after which the foul perpetrators marched off to their lines, satisfied that the wrath of their fallen deities was appeased by the bloody deed.

story says about these stones. Some antiquaries might suppose the "Seven Stanes" to have been, in former times, a Druidical place of worship; but tradition contradicts this, in a manner so distinct and pointed, that none, in any way acquainted with the connection which, in Scotland in particular, exists between oral testimony and written records, but must be struck with the plausibility of the story which tradition affords, and if not disposed to yield implicit confidence to all the details—must at least be ready to allow that it is worthy of being wrested from that oblivion to which most of our venerable tales of flood and field are rapidly hastening.

The "Seven Stanes" then, instead of being the remains of a Druidical place of worship, tradition informs us, are intended to commemorate a glorious victory obtained by an army of Scottish patriots under Wallace over an English army 10,000 strong, who were taken by surprise and cut to pieces. Wallace, who was not less remarkable for the celerity of his movements than the strength of his arm, determined not only to intercept it, but formed, at the same time, the most daring plan of cutting off their retreat, as if already assured of victory. For this purpose he divided his brave followers into three divisions; one of which he despatched in the night to the "Seven Stanes" —another was stationed at the Blackhill of Pendreigh, to fall upon the rear—and Wallace himself, with his division, lay on the Muir of Whiteheadston.

The English army, as Wallace had been previously led to believe, early on the following morning, after the Scottish dispositions were made, ascended the Sheriff-muir from Stirling; and such had been the secrecy and despatch with which the Scots had been assembled and arranged by their immortal leader, that one-half of their enemies were annihilated before being enabled to display almost a shadow of resistance, so completely were they surprised. Not even dreaming of the possibility of an enemy being at hand, these devoted men, marching on in straggling detachments, were suddenly and simultaneously assailed by the several Scottish divisions. That stationed near the "Seven Stanes" attacking the most advanced detachment, drove it back on the next in an instant; and following this advantage with furious impetuosity, all retreated before them in confusion and dismay. Precisely in a similar manner did the division at Pendreigh fall upon the rear, carrying all before *them* with a dreadful slaughter; while the mighty Wallace himself, with his followers, dealt death and destruction along the whole line of the converging retreat —and the several Scottish divisions latterly communicating with each other, and forming a semi-circular line, the vast group of fugitives, in utter confusion, was hemmed in, and a practicable retreat for them rendered desperate, on the dale where the "Stan'in' Stanes" were afterwards erected.

Here, we are told, the English, aware too late of their desperate situation, made a most determined effort to force the Scottish line, in order to secure a retreat (there being no other way than by a deep ravine close to the Ochils behind them—a retreat by which would have been to them immediate destruction), but the hatred of England, and heroic bravery of this valiant host overcoming all opposition, they were at last totally surrounded, and slain to a man. At "the Spout of Reiver-burn," and at the foot of "the Blackhill of Balhaldie," the carnage is related to have been terrible; and at "Harperstone," where Wallace's own division first fell upon the enemy, more than five hundred were cut off, surrounded, and speared, while he lost not a single man. To perpetuate this signal victory over his *Suthron* foe, Wallace caused "the Stan'in' Stanes" to be erected—and they furnish irresistible evidence of their being monuments of antiquity. The "Seven Stanes" were placed at the same time, and for the same purpose, as were also the "Muckle Stane o' Whiteston," and the "Great Stane" of Pendreigh.

II.

"THE AULD LAIRD O' BALHALDIE,"
CHIEF OF THE M'GREGORS.

" The Laird o' Balhaldie was there wi' his men,
Determin'd to conquer, or sleep wi' the slain ;
He drew his claymore at the dawn o' the day—
Tore from him the scabbard, an' threw it away."

"Auld Balhaldy, he was there, to haud the Whigs in order."
Old " Shirra-Moor " Songs.

THE M'Gregors, after the proscription of their name, seem to have broken down under new surnames, into several sub-divisive septs, which were headed by Chieftains ; while the *Kean Kinnhe* or Chief felt himself under the necessity of discarding the *Pine*, and assuming the name and badge of the Drummonds. Alexander Drummond, " the Auld Laird o' Balhaldie," and subject of these traditional memoirs, was allowed to be the lineal representative of the founder of the MacGregors. He is acknowledged as such in a letter to him, still extant, written by the celebrated Rob Roy.* And in those days he was unquestionably THE chief of the name.

"The Auld Laird," say our oral authorities, was a massy-built athletic man, of extraordinary agility for his weight, and a most expert broad-sword player. He was brave, and although of a passionate hasty temper, and consequently liable to be roused to the highest fury to resent an injury, yet we are told his enmity was of short duration, and that to those who would succumb to his sword he was merciful and generous. His known genealogy, habits, and disposition, naturally led him to assume the bearing and style of a Chief—more so, indeed, than his property, although respectable, could well maintain ; he was, however, in every respect, wisely frugal, and, like a careful farmer, superintended *himself* the cultivation of that portion of his

---

* In the possession of John Murray, Esq. of Livilands.

estates which he retained "in his own hand." He went
about the operations of his farm dressed generally in a suit
of "hodden-gray," with a broad blue bonnet; but on *high*
occasions he appeared in the garb of Rob Roy, whom, it is
said, out of courtesy to that Chieftain's warlike accomplishments and generosity, he sometimes acknowledged as
his Chief. He died at a very advanced age, so late as
1749 or 1750; and the following anecdotes of him are at
this day partially current among the older tenantry of
Balhaldie estate.

The Laird, it is universally allowed, was one of the
most devoted partisans of the House of Stewart. Of him
it might truly be said, he was the "bravest of the brave."
Knowing no fear, he was of the very foremost, and most
daring, although a mere youth, at the Battle of Killiecrankie—and at Sheriff-muir none were more conspicuously
brave. The death-blows dealt by him at Killiecrankie are
said to have been so numerous and terrible that upwards
of twenty fell under his claymore. At Sheriff-muir his
blows are reported to have been equally fatal. He was,
however, among the retreating division in that action; but
he disputed every inch of ground with his foe, till most of
his vassals and tenantry who rallied around him were
numbered with the slain. Unable to resist the force of
numbers, he was latterly, singly and alone, under the
necessity of taking shelter at his own mansion-house, which
stood within a mile of the line of retreat. Thither he had
been followed by some dragoons, who, seeing him unat-
tended, made sure of their victim; and justly, wounded as
he was, and with such odds against him, had he not been
so fortunate as to succeed in saving his life by throwing
himself into his own "kail-yard," where he lay concealed
among "the lang green-kail," until the attention of the
pursuing party was directed otherwise. Luckily this
detached party of Argyll's dragoons had been perceived
by a retreating party of Stair's horse, who, quickly rallying,

attacked them with the utmost fury, and in a few moments annihilated them, horse and man. This affair happened near to the spot where Balhaldie Inn now stands. The heroic warrior at last rose from his uncomfortable place of concealment, with the sword still in his grasp, naked and bloody, as when he first left the battle-ground. He found himself so weak, benumbed, and stiff, from the excessive fatigue he had undergone, that it was with difficulty he could walk upright,—and his hand had so much swollen in the basket of his broad-sword that part of the iron frame-work had to be removed by the file before it could be disengaged from the blood-dyed weapon.

Upon learning the fate of his tenantry, who, with one exception, were all slain, the Laird is asserted to have almost sunk entirely under excessive grief. They had been all taught by *himself* the use of the broad-sword, and were devoted to him and his interests, which they accounted their own, and had died in his defence. One of these, in particular, the Laird lamented with sorrow of the deepest description—William M'Gregor, of Lang-bank. This man had attained to such proficiency in the warlike accomplishments of his Clan, that the Laird even allowed him to be superior to himself. He was shot in the very act of warding off a sabre-stroke from the head of his master, at the commencement of the battle.

In the Laird's younger years a feud existed between himself and a neighbouring proprietor—the Laird of Feddal. This Feddal was reported the *ne plus ultra* of the district in the management of the Highland broadsword, so dexterously adept that he could measure his distance-point in a manner so very exact as to "*cut the button from the shirt-neck of an antagonist without injuring his person.*" Baldhaldie could ill brook the idea being entertained that a "better man" existed than himself at the broad-sword. It was his favourite weapon of war—he practised it from childhood, and never had in bloody strife met his equal. In order, as he said, to settle differences for *ever*, then existing between himself and the Laird of Feddal, he challenged the Laird to single combat—sword and targe. The challenge being accepted, the parties met on the banks of the Allan, below Greenloaning, when a desperate combat ensued, which continued upwards of an hour. The combatants by this time were both slightly wounded, but neither seemed to have the least advantage of his antagonist—only Balhaldie, being the stronger man, was expected to hold longest out. At this critical moment the false blade of Feddal gave way at the hilt, and he, expecting to be instantly stabbed to the heart, sprang back, and bared his breast to the foe. But Balhaldie was as generous as he was brave; and respecting, to a high degree of enthusiasm, all whom he found adepts in the use of his favourite weapon, instantly checked himself, and casting his sword and targe to the ground, threw his arms around the man with whom he had just been engaged in deadly strife, and, warmly embracing him, begged that henceforth they might be friends. He at the same time declared that all he had heard of his opponent's prowess must be true, since his own life was never till that moment in danger. Feddal returned a similar compliment to the dexterity of Balhaldic's sword-arm, and from that moment the rival sword players, instead of being jealous and inveterate enemies, became united in the bonds of indissoluble friendship.

In those days the celebrated Rob Roy was the tutelary guardian of the live-stock of all those in Strathallan, as well as in many other districts, who chose to pay him *black-mail*. Balhaldie being Chief of Rob's Clan was protected *gratis*, but Feddal (who had lately become one of his most intimate friends), from the proximity of his hill-grounds to the Highlands, being on the north side of Strathallan, and consequently more exposed to the predatory excursions of northern *cattle-lifters*, paid a heavy tax.

Through Balhaldie's influence this tax was modified; yet Feddal fell in arrears, being either unable or unwilling to pay. One evening, about Michaelmas, Balhaldie being on a visit at Feddal-house,—while the two Lairds were carousing, and telling of blows and broad-swords, notice was brought that the whole cattle on Feddal-moor were *lifted* and driven off. Instantly the two Lairds, vowing death and destruction, accoutred themselves for the rescue, and, mounting their horses, galloped off in pursuit, scarcely taking leisure to leave the necessary instructions for their tenantry to *rise* and follow. Overtaking the marauders, as the morning dawned, at Glenartney, a bloody conflict ensued, in which Balhaldie slew seven with his own hand, but had his horse killed under him, and received himself several wounds in the affray. On looking around, after all was over, he perceived his friend Feddal in imminent danger. This gentleman had, at the first onset, come in contact with the leader of the *lifters*, a robust mountaineer from Glenlyon—well accoutred, and on horse-back. Both their horses lay dead beside them, while they fought on foot, hand to hand. Balhaldie hastened, as fast as his wounds permitted, to assist his friend, but ere he could effect his object, he observed, on the heights above, the whole tenantry on Feddal estate advancing, armed with hay-forks, scythes, swords, and other weapons. Balhaldie, on arriving at the spot, called to the Highlander to *give in*, and he should have his life. Hearing the shouts of the motley group of tenantry, and taking one glance at them, he threw down his sword. Feddal knowing from experience what a brave man he had encountered, prevailed upon him to accompany him to Strathallan, and gave him a pendicle of land free of rent, during his life.

But this affray had signally incensed Rob Roy. The redoubtable mountaineer of Glenlyon had been employed by him to make reprisals on all such as neglected or refused to pay *black-mail* within the boundaries of *his* jurisdiction. He soon got notice of the discomfiture of his substitute, and the slaughter of his armed assistants in the dales of Glenartney—for scarcely had the two Lairds, with the tenantry, the hero of Glenlyon, and the recovered cattle, arrived at Feddal, than Rob Roy, with a band of his followers, was at hand. The Lairds had just sat down to talk over the events of the day, and dress their wounds, when a horn blew, and on looking out they observed the banner of Rob Roy streaming in the moon-beams, and the house nearly surrounded by armed men. Tradition does not, however, furnish us with the particulars of the sequel. We are merely informed that through Balhaldie's influence the wrath of Rob Roy was appeased, and a remission of the tax imposed on Feddal under the name of *black-mail* obtained, after a carousal which lasted until the following morning, when "Rab and his men" again betook themselves towards their fastnesses.

III.

THE M'GREGORS AND "THE SHIRRA-MOOR."

EARLY on the forenoon of that day on which the armies under the Earl of Mar and Duke of Argyll met in deadly strife on the heights of Sheriff-muir, Rob Roy, with some five hundred of the flower of his Clan, were observed, by the shepherds and solitary cottagers of the heath, hurriedly traversing those pathless and irregular wilds which stretch betwixt the small villages of Kinbuck and Callander. Brushing the new-fallen snow-flakes from the heath, "the M'Gregors" rushed eastwards at a rapid pace, until arriving at a place called "Bent of Cullins," where Rob suddenly halted his girded warriors, as if to await the issue of the approaching fray, at a distance of about four miles. From this place "Rab and his men" would readily perceive every movement of the northern host, previous to its collision with the "red-coats;" and, according to tradition, they had only remained a short time at "the Bent" when they observed the Highland lines, " dark and deep," steadily ascend the northern side of the opposite moor. " The Clans " having shortly attained the summit of the height, no sooner was this accomplished than a loud and terrific yell announced to " the M'Gregors " that furious onset of their countrymen, which proved irresistible and became instantly victorious. On hearing the wild war-cry of " the Clans," at the moment of attack, we are told that Rob's followers, as it were involuntarily, drew every man his sword, exhibiting those symptoms of furious agitation and fiery impatience peculiar to Highland warriors on exciting occasions. But when, shortly afterwards, they beheld the *defeated* wing, under every disadvantage slowly retiring, and disputing the ground inch by inch, their distress was extreme ; they demanded to be led on to its assistance, with entreaties—nay, it is said, with tears—but their Chieftain was inexorable, and their tears and entreaties were in vain.

What Rob's original intention was in this descent has, perhaps, never been clearly ascertained, although tradition will, that his sole object was plunder. On assembling the flower of his name he may have had no specific object in view, intending merely to be guided by circumstances. On this memorable day it was undoubtedly in his power, from the position he had chosen at Bent, to join either belligerent at any time of the engagement, having here free communication with both armies—that of the Duke, by Dunblane Bridge, and of the Earl by Kinbuck Ford. Both previous to, and during the battle, we have the best oral testimony for stating that this cautious and intrepid Chieftain had overtures from both Commanders, earnestly courting his assistance, with large promises, all which were finally rejected. Rob, indeed, is said to have remained long undecided, walking backwards and forwards on the heath ; and that his reply to the last message sent him by Argyll was that the M'Gregors would, if they did fight that day, fight against none but red-coats. Oral story also says that Rob "sounded his men" in the following manner :— Standing before them, he asked them, "Would they fight for M'Callamore ?" Every head hung down. "Then," said the Chieftain, "Will you fight for my Lord Mar ?" when, in an instant, every sword was gleaming from its scabbard. "But," said Rob, "*I* will fight for neither the one nor the other. Let us strike in at the close for King *Spulzie*—be victor who will, *we* shall have the spoil." He added that the Duke of Argyll and the Earl of Mar were equally his *friends*, and he should leave them to decide *it* themselves.

Part of the very words of Mar's last message to Rob Roy, earnestly soliciting him to assist the Highlanders, seem to be preserved in the "The Highlanders' Prayer[*] at the battle of Sheriff-muir," as recorded by Burns, who, no doubt, had the original from his "hostess" in Dunblane. Mar, in conclusion, said that if he could not possibly prevail on Rob to render assistance to his countrymen, he begged that he would remain neutral, and "leave it between the red-coats and us." Rob, in very deed, and we shall say to his dishonour, *did* remain "neutral" and inactive during this bloody affray, and "in the eye" of the several combatants, with a force sufficient to have turned the tide of battle decidedly in favour of the Jacobites, had he thought proper to rush to the assistance of his kinsman, the Laird of Balhaldie, and other leaders of the retreating wing, while defending themselves so obstinately in their slow retrogression through the moor.

At the close of the fight, continue our oralists, from the circumstance of the victorious wing of the Highlanders

---

[*] This "Prayer," as given by the Poet, runs thus :—"O L--d, *be* wi' us—but if thou be *not* wi' us—be *not against* us—but leave *it* betwixt the red-coats and us."

occupying the field of battle during the greater part of the night, and the Duke's army the City of Dunblane, insurmountable obstacles were thus interposed betwixt the M'Gregors and the slain, and they in consequence shared none of the booty. Tradition informs us of strong parties of the M'Gregors being sent to the neighbouring farmers and cotters of Cromlix, to procure provisions in the evening after "the battle;" and an amusing anecdote is told of the reception one of these had from "the gudewife of Hutchieston," who would not *sell* her gear on the Sabbath-day. The party found, at this place, every door and window secured, but having strict authority from their Chieftain, durst use no violence. They threatened to bombard and burn; but Lucky said, if they were really Rob Roy's men, they "durstna do either the tane or the tither." Knowing there were plenty of provisions in the house, the party despatched some of their number to their master, desiring to know how they should act, and Rob was on the spot instantly in person. "Open your door," said the Chieftain, "we will do you no harm. We want some refreshment, for which we will pay." "Just gae ye're ways," said the gudewife, "I tell ye it wad be a cryin' sin to *sell* on the Lord's day." "Weel, mistress," replied Rob Roy, "as sure as my name is Rob Roy, if you do not open, I shall not leave you a cock to craw, nor a soul to be saved, ere the morning light;" and even quoted Scripture to do away the good woman's scruples, which were certainly more fictitious than real on this occasion. In a word, we are told, admittance was immediately had afterwards, and stores of provisions were given to the party to carry to their kinsmen; for which Rob, to save any demurs of conscience in the mind of this female Whig, amply paid for all in a purse of money, presented by him to one of the woman's children, who "in it's fecket, ere a' was done, was admiring the bonny things on Rob Roy's sword."

IV.

ANECDOTES OF THE BATTLE OF SHERIFF-MUIR.

13TH NOVEMBER, 1715.

1st.—On the day of this memorable battle almost every Highlander bore a "wallet" of oatmeal on his back for subsistence. The meal-bags of those that were slain being collected after the battle, they were emptied on a carpeting of tartan plaids, spread for the purpose, and tradition records that the whole amounted to many bolls —such was the number of the hardy sons of the north who were this day sacrificed.

2d.—Some shepherds, who witnessed the battle from one of the Ochils, ("Little-Hunt-Hill,") observed a considerable party of "red-coats" cut off, and surrounded by a strong body of Clans. The "red-coats" appeared to them at first, in the centre of the Clans, in the form of a "red diamond," which gradually diminished in size, until it became totally extinct—not a man being spared by those merciless wielders of the dreadful claymore.

3d.—An old woman, then residing at the farm-house of Linns, in the immediate vicinity of the scene, used to tell that she saw eleven "red-coats" killed on her own "midden"—the poor fellows defending themselves to the last,—the Highland party then entering the house with their bloody swords still unsheathed, carried off every thing which they found valuable, or which they deemed of use to them—some of them declaring that they fought neither for "King Shordy nor King Hamish, but for King *Spulzie*."

4th.—During the dispersion of the left wing of the Royal Army, one Highlander, with a large uncovered curly head, having his plaid wrapt round his arm to ward off the bayonets, is said to have cut down nine individuals before he was overpowered; and, on the other hand, a single dragoon is related to have been chased through the bogs, to a stone dyke at Wharrie-burn, by a dozen of Highlanders, where he defended himself so well that no fewer than ten men fell under his arm before he was discomfited and slain.

5th.—*The Shepherd o' Braco.*—This man is related to have been trained from his infancy to the use of the broad-sword—to have been most fierce and robust, and more than ordinarily attached to scenes of strife and bloodshed. In his youth he had repeatedly foiled parties of Highland *harryers*, who had descended from the hills during the "Michaelmas moons" to plunder those Lowlanders who like himself resided in the neighbourhood of their fastnesses, and had slain several of them in single combat. Armed with two-handed swords, this heroic "tender of the flocks," with two other resolute adherents of the fallen dynasty, descended from "Langside" on the evening before the battle—managed afterwards to be foremost in the fray, and in the victorious wing of the Highlanders. Bearing down all opposition in the onset, these three men gave chase to a broken party of dragoons, seven in number. Pursuing them to a deep ravine in Pendreigh-glen, they saw farther retreat was impracticable for the horsemen, and made sure of their annihilation, as they had the greatest confidence in the individual prowess of each other. "Two to one" was considered nothing by these doughty men, and they immediately made the attack with their terrible two-handed swords. Three dragoons fell in a moment, for, strange to say, although they all fired their pistols, none of the balls took effect. But the other four made a desperate resistance, and in a few minutes more not a living man stood upright but the "Shepherd of Braco." The spot where the *nine* men were buried is marked by a large stone, in a little haugh of the Wharrie, about a mile above the "Loup o' Pendreigh."

V.

DUNBLANE ANECDOTES OF THE "FORTY-FIVE."

No. I.—THE HIGHLAND ARMY.

THAT Prince Charles Edward, in the *insurrection* of 1745, proved himself a genuine scion of the royal and illustrious line of Stewart—a youth of the most daring martial genius, not unworthy of the greatest of his ancestors—none will deny. Every incident, therefore, connected with this Prince and his warlike adherents, in their short but brilliant career of glory, will be interesting to those who delight to cherish the memorable achievements of our forefathers, in favour of that unfortunate but legitimate name. The following are merely gleanings from " the events of a night," in Dunblane and immediate neighbourhood. They are, however, well authenticated by tradition.

In the afternoon of the 12th September, 1745, the Prince arriving at Dunblane with the main body of his Highlanders, cantoned in and about the village for the night. The town was, of course, inundated with motley groups of those mountaineers, who, believing themselves in the midst of their enemies—all the efforts of their superior officers were totally inadequate to restrain many from indulging in their plundering propensities. Subalterns are said to have been as much addicted to pillage as privates, and not a few who were designated lieutenants and captains were known to have winked at the theftuous outrages of those under their command, notwithstanding that the Prince had, under severe penalties, enjoined his followers to abstain from all predatory warfare. Something, indeed, in the shape of a provo-marshal—" an auld man wi' kilt and tap-boots, mountit on a black heelan filly "—enforced a semblance of order on the streets ; and officers might be seen applying the flat sides of their swords

to the shoulders of those whom they observed darting from
shops and houses with more than could be readily concealed of "progues," bonnets, hams, and other *spulzie*—
but much private loss was sustained by the inhabitants,
for very little was paid for. Most dexterously adept at
purloining were they—and no *hidden treasure* escaped the
vigilance of their eyes, or the probes of their swords.
Many farm-houses in the neighbourhood were pillaged,
and some completely sacked. The predilection for cream
was general—" ta pooter, ta sheese, and ta *ream-crowty* "
(cream mixed with oatmeal) was the perpetual call of
party after party. "Crowty" was preferred by most to
every other sort of food—and few refused to pay for
" crowty "—but when the means of gratifying their appetites with this species of "meats" were exhausted they
raved and stormed, and sometimes maltreated. A wellfilled *kirn* once obtained, to prevent surprise they would
remove from the house to the nearest knoll, where, in the
manner of "hoody-craws" they devoured their prey at
leisure. One of those *kirns* was discovered in a suburbhouse of the village. On this, the discoverer hinting the
matter to a few select companions, the door was forthwith
barred against the rest of the party until "ta clorious
meats" was gulped. In this brief interval some *without*
having their suspicions as to what was going on within,
endeavoured to force the door with their weapons—but
all was *down* before a breach could be effected. This door
is still "creaking on its old hinges," on which the muzzlemarks of the Highland muskets in this affair are shown
to this day.

A single Highlander at nightfall came to the solitary
cottage of a poor woman on Whiteheadston Moor. The
door was fastened, but he having declared he would burn
the house in case he were not admitted, the trembling old
creature at last undid the bar. It was of no use her telling him that she was poor—in want of even the necessaries

of life—he entirely disregarded her tale of pity. Commencing a rummage among her old furniture he found a small *kebbuck*, which he immediately appropriated, and preparing his wallet, began to make a transference of her "wee puckle meal." Her "meal-barrel" was nearly empty, but it was deep, and had seen better days. The old woman, in tears of despair, at thus seeing her *all* taken from her by ruthless hands, watching her opportunity while Donald was "half-in half-out" of the barrel, seized him suddenly by the limbs, completely overbalanced him, and, in a phrenzy of desperation, maintained the devoted wretch in that position until life was utterly extinct.

A party, after dusk, were in the act of plundering the farm-house of Lendrick, when an old man, in the garb of his kinsmen, suddenly appeared in the bustle of the ransack, conjuring his countrymen in their native language to desist. "Thirty years ago," said he, "in this house I found an asylum. Severely wounded by Argyll's men within a mile of the spot whereon I stand, with the greatest difficulty I made this length, craved protection, and craved it not in vain. At the hazard of his fortune, and perhaps his life, the good man of this house saved *my* life, and concealed my retreat. Harm not this roof, then, I entreat you!" The old warrior's words had the effect of electricity. The ruthless marauders launched into the most glowing expressions of gratitude, restored every man that which he had already pillaged, declaring that there "were always some *friends* in an *enemy's* country;" and in order to protect the house from the ravages of others of their men, the party bivouacked in and about the premises.

The Prince himself lodged at a house in the village, the property of an adherent—Alexander Drummond, Esq. of Balhaldie. A messenger arrived at a late hour at the Prince's quarters, with intelligence for the Laird, intimating that a party of robbers following the army were plundering his tenants on Balhaldie estates, and wantonly hanging those who made a show of resistance. Obtaining permission from his Prince, Young Balhaldie selected twelve of his body-guard, and at their head galloped off, full speed, to punish the transgressors. On entering the threshold of his father's mansion-house, his senses were shocked and confounded at the scene which presented itself. Some of the servants lay bound and streaming with blood, others suspended by the heels from the kitchen-*bauks* dangled there in a state of delirium; the other apartments of the house, meanwhile, resounding to the fierce disputatious hagglings, held in Gaelic, about the respective value of several articles of plunder, which the robbers were packing into their "habbersacks" with all possible despatch. Attached, as he was, to the cause of the Prince, this act of lawless insubordination roused alike the Young Laird's indignation and his wrath. The fellows were so incumbered with their spoils, and young Drummond and his party set upon them so warmly, that they had no time to ward off the death-blows which immediately fell heavily among them. Tradition says the havoc was so dreadful that not a man of them escaped, and even points out a place called Burnside Glen as the spot where the whole were buried.

A serious circumstance followed. The servants being released from their hempen fetters, one of them approached the now prostrate Gaels, writhing in the last agonies of death, to whom, without resistance, he had submitted to be bound, and bearing a poker, which he had now collected courage to use, he aimed a heavy blow at the head of one of the dying men, observing, at the same time, that "half-a-dizzen wadna hae managed that deevil when he cam here, but he could noo *kill* a hale dizzen o' him himsel." Drummond is said to have been so much incensed at this dastardly action that, in the heat of rage and passion, the unsheathed sword which he had been using in defence of his vassal was now turned upon himself, and in an instant struck the base wretch lifeless to the earth—Drummond ordering his corpse to be buried—not among his kindred —but along with the marauders to be deposited in Burnside Glen.

During his short stay of twenty-four hours in Dunblane, Prince Charles was visited by different distinguished persons of both sexes, wholly devoted to his cause. Among these was a Mrs. Bailie Russell, of the Keavil family. She pressed him to accept, at her hands, a purse of gold, while, with tears in her eyes, she bade him "God speed," at same time fervently expressing a wish that she were herself of the other sex, to follow his banners and share his fortunes.

The waiting maid at "Balhaldie House," who was a fine handsome young woman, had drunk deeply of the devotion which had bound her master's family to the Prince's fortunes. The duty of presenting the young Prince, before his departure, with clean boots having fallen to this young damsel's office, and the Prince remarking that her countenance was sorrowful and overcast—rallied her to keep her spirits up—that they would soon be back again, after they had made friends of their enemies. The generous girl, in an ecstasy of enthusiasm— not daring to lay hold on the hand which the Prince had stretched out in his haste to receive the boots—silently kissed one of the latter; and with her eyes suffused in tears, wished "God speed him," but with prophetic despondency, added, alluding to his enemies—"Ah! my Prince, my Prince, *but there's ten to one against you.*"

No. II.—"DUKE WILLIAM'S ARMY."

THE Highland army, under their enterprising leader, had not left Dunblane above an hour when the ears of her citizens were stunned with the noise of an irregular cannonade from the batteries of Stirling Castle, and it was at first believed that Prince Charles had changed his intended route by the Fords of Frew, and was at that moment threatening to effect a passage to the south at Kildeanford, a short way above Stirling. The truth speedily turned out to be that numerous groups of the Clans having separated from the main body betwixt Dunblane and Doune, were then scouring the carses of Lecropt, Greenock, and those to the westward, exacting contributions or foraging for provisions, while General Blackney was discharging his crazy cannon, of a few grosses of round shot, and some barrels of gunpowder, to intimidate the Highlanders. Numbers of the iron balls at this time discharged have within the last thirty years been dug up, in clearing away the "Moss of Lecropt." But let us hasten to our subject.

Prince Charles and his gallant and intrepid Highlanders had, as is well known, no sooner gained the signal victory of Tranent—after penetrating with his handful of warriors to the centre of England, and paralysing the councils around the very throne—and subsequently accomplishing one of the most masterly retreats ever achieved since the days of Xenophon, and defeating with great slaughter an equal if not superior force of his recreant enemy on Falkirk Moor—than he found himself, from the pressure of accumulating numbers in his rear, and other causes more alarming, under the necessity of retreating to those fastnesses where the greater part of his warlike adherents had issued only a few months before. This now dispirited but unsubdued little host was retiring through Dunblane in detached, gloomy, and silent clumps, but in perfect order, to the deafening notes of their natonal music, while his Grace of Cumberland was "dragging his slow length along" some miles south of Stirling.

Early in the forenoon of 4th February, 1746, the advanced guard of the Royal army, in passing through Dunblane for Crieff, left letters for the proper authorities, intimating that the Duke, with the main body, would arrive there that evening. The then Regality Bailie

(Russell), who had " a' the say " about that place in those days, was in a mighty bustle on receiving this notice. This man was a loyal, zealous, and upright Whig—but his wife, his *better*-half, was exactly the reverse. His mansion was, in modern ideas, the most respectable and best furnished Whig domicile of the city—and where, thought the Bailie, could " his Royal Highness" pass the night so well as under his roof, although he trembled at the idea, lest in that case the unbending cavalier-spirit of his spouse should betray her into some frightful extravagance, for he had heard her declare she would, with her own hands, poinard the "base German" that instant the threshold of her door was darkened by his shadow. The Bailie had, in these troublesome times, only one coadjutor in whom he could repose implicit confidence—the Rev. Mr. Simpson of the place. This man's character is handed down to us as one of the most amiable description. In religion he was a true and unbigoted reformer—a man who deplored the miseries of his country—yet felt an honest partiality towards the House of Stuart, as the true and legitimate heirs of the British throne. Through this gentleman's influence the obduracy of Mrs. Russell's temper was mollified for a time, she having consented that the Duke should be entertained that night in her house, provided her husband's invitation was accepted. The Bailie and Minister had lost no time in calling a general meeting of the inhabitants—for no sooner were those little domestic affairs arranged betwixt the Minister and Mr. Russell, than on these two gentlemen approaching the Cross they were eagerly saluted by a dense assemblage, comprising most of the population of the town. The Bailie immediately mounted the Tolbooth Stair, harrangued the multitude, conjuring them, as the safest course, "always to be subject to the powers that be," whatever were their opinions and prejudices; and he begged of them, as they valued their own safety—the honour and protection of their wives and children, to give the "royal army" a friendly reception. He was followed by Mr. Simpson with the happiest effect. "Smarting as they must be," said this gentleman, "after repeated defeats, the royal army will treat us all as rebels, provided we be so foolish as hazard our all by throwing any obstruction in their way. I therefore propose that every male amongst us march out and welcome the Duke of Cumberland to Dunblane. We can lose nothing by succumbing thus far—and we may lose much by doing otherwise." The Minister was aware that there were many fierce Jacobites in the place—and he had just learned, that in attempting to pillage "Ardoch House," seven miles north of Dunblane, the advanced guard had a number of men shot from the windows before they accomplished their purpose. This was the first Cavalier's mansion that was robbed by the southern army north of the Forth.

To return. The greater part having acceded to the Minister's proposition, they sallied out along the bridge to "welcome the Duke," the two gentlemen leading the way. About a mile south of the town, at a place called the Skelly Braes, the Bailie "called a halt," and after arranging the crowd on each side of the road, in something like files, concerted a signal that his Grace might be saluted with a simultaneous huzza as soon as he and his staff arrived at a certain position betwixt the motley lines. The Duke having shortly afterwards made his appearance, "surrounded with his principal officers," almost in the van of his army, the Bailie's signal-flag was hoisted, and the air resounded to long and continued cheers. With this at least equivocal token of attachment to his "father's House," his Grace is said to have been much pleased, and to have remarked to an officer that stood by that he had been told *all* were rebels north of the Forth, but there was certainly one exception at least. The Bailie and his friend having stepped up and paid their respects, the whole moved onward towards the town, and the Duke, followed by his travelling equipage, and a few officers, accompanied the Bailie to his house, to pass the night. Part of the army was disposed through the city—the rest encamped around the baggage and artillery on the Crofts, immediately south of the bridge, now laid off in feus, and appropriated as the minister's glebe.

The Duke, on arriving at the Bailie's mansion, was of course shown into the best room—not by Mrs. Russell however, but by the Bailie himself. Armed sentinels were instantly placed at every avenue and at every door of the house. At that passage which led to the room appropriated and fitted up for "his Grace," five sentinels stood without, and two within the door, with loaded muskets and fixed bayonets. At these precautionary measures the Bailie was not a little vexed and chagrined, for he deemed such things unnecessary about his house. But when, *sans ceremonie*, he witnessed the bustle of a number of attendants with the Duke's portable bedstead, bedding, *sackets* of provisions and cooking utensils, the simple honest man was astounded, and could not help murmuring even to Mrs. Russell that so little confidence should be reposed in him that had "always favoured the House of Hanover, and the Protestant succession." Mrs. Russell only replied with a bitter sneer of contempt, saying, "Cowards and usurpers are aye carefu' o' their *ain carcases*, and these *only*." The Duke, after supping with his principal officers, and cracking a few bottles of wine—all from his own commissariat—took a nap in his own bedding, after which he got up pretty early to issue orders to his army. He found, however, that some small matters had necessarily to be adjusted before he himself started,—he therefore ordered the march to be sounded, while he himself sat in judgment upon a few delinquents. A man, by trade a tailor, belonging to Kilbryde, had been caught prowling about an out-post baggage waggon, after having succeeded in abstracting a weighty Gloucester cheese, which, it would appear, had not satiated his covetousness; and he, looking about for another opportunity of adding something more to what he had already acquired, was taken. The Duke ordered him to be hanged over the bridge, but by the interposition of the Bailie he was pardoned. Two others were detected and apprehended in the act of pillaging from an ammunition waggon. Their names were M'Niven and Brown. "Let the *Mack* be hanged," said the Duke summarily; "but *Brown*—Brown," he repeated, "We have many *Browns* in the army—let *him* be set at liberty." Our traditionary oracles do not agree as to the fate of M'Niven. Some will have it that he was actually suspended from the then low parapets of the bridge; others that his life was also saved by the timely interference of either the Bailie or Mr. Simpson.

A bullock and a draught horse were stolen from the church-yard, where those cattle were provendered for the night, but the delinquents had been fortunate enough to elude the vigilance of the guard in removing their booty; and the church-yard fence, at that time scarcely deserving the name, having favoured their design, no traces of the animals were for a long time discovered. The depredators, were, however, afterwards well known. They used to term it "lawful prey," adding that they only regretted they did not succeed in blowing up an ammunition waggon, which they were very nearly effecting. Upon learning the latter act of theft the Duke felt quite indignant, and it was believed that had it been brought first before him the tailor, Brown, and M'Niven, would all have inevitably and instantly suffered death.

These matters arranged, the Duke prepared to follow the rear of his army, which was by this time some miles on its way. The horse he rode is said to have been a beautiful grey, and richly caparisoned. No sooner, however, had he mounted his charger, and advanced about fifty yards, than an incident happened, which, had the design been fully accomplished, the cold-blooded, cruel, and barbarous massacres which followed the battle of Culloden, had, in all probability, never occurred. His Grace, with his officers and guard, while passing an ancient building, now uninhabited and in a dilapidated state, then the property of Lord Strathallan, and yet well known in Dunblane by the appellation of "My Lord's House," very narrowly escaped being scalded to death by a pail of boiling oil, which was poured from an attic window of this house, directly over him. So near was the burning liquid of having the intended effect, that the whole fell right on the haunches of the Duke's horse, which suddenly starting from the excessive pain, darted in a moment from below his rider, and left him weltering in the mud.

During the confusion occasioned by this circumstance, the girl who had been instigated to commit this daring action, from "love to the righteous cause," and hatred to "the usurper," found means to escape from the house, and secreted herself in a tunnel which conveyed the filth of the town below ground to the brink of the river. This was the same girl who had shown so much devotion to the cause of Prince Charles at Balhaldie House, when presenting him with clean boots some four or five months previous. The most diligent search was made for her in and about the mansion, but in vain. Every door was forced, and every corner rummaged, but all to no purpose, while the Bailie stood wringing his hands, expecting every moment to hear the order given to lay the town in ashes. It is believed that the girl was prompted to the execution of this plot by some young ladies relatives of Lord Strathallan, then residing in the house; but they stoutly protesting that they knew nothing of it, and assuming every appearance of innocence, the Duke and his attendants were easily deceived, and no violence was offered. Balhaldie himself was reported to have been accessory to this affair—nay, that with him the design originated, and that he had instructed his maid to repair to "My Lord's House," on pretence of seeing "his Grace," but really with a different purpose, as the event shewed. The town would have been burnt, say some of our oralists, but for the Bailie's interference and the genuine eloquence of Mr. Simpson. Others relate that the Duke gave out at his departure, that nothing else than a promise which had been extorted from him by the Bishop of York, on his way to Scotland, not to injure Dunblane, prevented him from razing it to the ground. Be this as it may, Dunblane got rid of the Duke and his army with fully as little *scaith* as could reasonably have been expected.

During the night different affrays happened betwixt the citizens and soldiers on the streets. A daring Jacobite fired a gun at midnight at the cross, proclaiming King James, and being suddenly seized by a couple of soldiers, fought a desperate battle, and ultimately levelled both his opponents with the butt-end of his gun, receiving himself two bayonet stabs in the scuffle. Two bluff Englishmen were billoted on an old Highlander, whose humble domicile was in the Mill Row. A bacon ham, which hung suspended from the *rantle-trees* having excited the gluttonous cupidity of these men, they offered him a certain sum for as much of it as they could eat for supper. The terms being agreed to, the ham was taken down, and a large portion of it duly sliced and prepared with *two dozen eggs*, which the two soldiers dispatched with a seeming comfort and voracity which astonished the simple Gael, who could not help observing, "at the close of the work," "Cot laats, you'll pe carry mhore in your pelly tan ta heelanman on him's pack. Gif you'll pe stay lang in ta heelans you'll pe neither leave ta soo an' ta negg, nor ta seet o' hims to growe at a'."

Two or three soldiers stepping into a smith's shop in the evening, having used indiscreet language to Vulcan, who was a very powerful man, he raised the hammer which was in his hand against the whole party, and succeeded in beating them to the floor of the smithy—then suddenly shutting his door and locking it upon the prostrate soldiers, he hastened to the Bailie, and craving an audience of the Duke, was admitted to his presence. He stated the bare truth—that the men had insulted his country, in language which no true Scotsman could brook—and that he had, in the excitement of the moment, levelled them with the earth, and confined them in his smithy, to know his Grace's pleasure. The Duke applauded his conduct, and ordered an officer to accompany him to ascertain the delinquents' names. Regarding particulars of the sequel, we only know that this smith was again attacked that very night by a numerous party of English, for the purpose of revenging the discomfiture and disgrace of their comrades, when Tranent, in miniature, was exhibited in gallant style. Vulcan, with a cast-iron pot upon his head, to defend his *crown*, and an old Ferrara in his hand, laid about him so lustily, that the cravens vanished in a twinkling—not, however, before some of them had reason to repent of their rashness in rousing the energies of this daring and powerful man.

One of the advanced guard, an Argyllshire Highlander, in passing through Dunblane, stepped into a cot-house of the suburbs "to warm himsel," it being, as he said, "very caul." The woman residing in this house, who piqued herself much upon her honesty and knowledge of the Bible, observing the poor man, who seemed a mere recruit, and to appearance but simple, cast a longing eye at the kail-pot "tottling on the fire," began a colloquy in the following terms:—" Pair body, will ye tak a wee drap broo to warm you?" He gave a fidge, saying, "she'll no be carin." After supping the *broo*, Lucky enquired whether he would taste the mutton. The same answer was given, "she'll no pe carin." During the time he was picking the rib which was given him, some conversation took place about the price of mutton in his country, when he said that they had no more ado than go to the hills and *lift* what was necessary. The woman now began, in no "measured mood," to expatiate on the heinousness of sheep-stealing, and made a few scripture quotations in support of her arguments. Donald heard her patiently, then looking her broad in the face, rejoined—"Mistress, if you'll pe reat ta screptar, you'll to a surely pe reat tere tat 'ta cattles on ta toosan hills are *mine.*'" This anecdote would not be worthy of record but for the sequel. This woman was then in the wane, and had nearly "lost hopes," but had scraped together some few pounds, with which she bought off her *lover* from the army—marched off with him to his native hills, and was not heard of for a long time, when she returning on a visit to her relatives in Dunblane, and described her *courtship* as related above.

If the Highland army was held in terror in its way south by the inhabitants of Dunblane, the English, on the other hand, were held in utter disgust and contempt. The recent defeats which they had experienced at the hands of the northern warriors had a powerful tendency in producing a feeling of confidence in Highland intrepidity, which, by the more sanguine, was thought would ultimately prove successful in effecting another restoration. What, it was asked, could be expected from men who so disgracedly fled at Tranent and Falkirk—and would not face a handful of enemies in the centre of their native country. The Scotch, we may say generally, were disgusted at the immoral character of the *Suthron* soldiery, and none more so than the citizens of Dunblane. Old prejudices might indeed have revived — but the horrible profanity of English oaths, and the voracity of their appetites for beef, bacon, and eggs, became afterwards proverbial. There were not wanting, moreover, many instances of paltry peculation committed by them during their one night's sojourn about Dunblane. Hams, in particular, disappeared most unaccountably in the confusion, and hen-roosts were everywhere untenanted around the bivouac on the Crofts. Although swine had been but lately introduced so far north, and pork was then still considered forbidden, and unlawful to be used as an article of food by "the law of Moses," it was remarked that the Englishmen seemed to relish it in the same degree that the Highlander did his humble but substantial "crowty." This created, of itself, not a little disgust; the old women used to say, "thae *gutsy* English mak' just *middens* o' their wames."

To conclude. It is notorious that the Duke of Cumberland winked at those outrages of his army while in Scotland, which Prince Charles, in England, vainly endeavoured to supress in his. The Highland army was poor and needy—this must plead some excuse. That of " his Grace " lacked for nothing—his therefore permitting the defenceless inhabitants, on his northern rout, to be maltreated by a brutal soldiery, and the mansions of the cavaliers to be plundered and burnt, without discrimination, can add little more to his honour than his permission of the dreadful excesses which followed the carnage of Culloden.

VI.

"AULD CALZIE."

JAMES STEWART, sheep-farmer at Calzie-Balhalzie, south base of Uwanvhore, who died about seventy years ago, inherited more than an ordinary portion of that martial spirit which was roused into action during the victories of Montrose, and which burned with true devotion in the heart of many a Highlander, in the several subsequent attempts to restore the Stewart family to the British throne. James Stewart, the hero of the present number of our Oral Traditions, was born at a humble cot on the banks of the Garry, and was about seven years old when his father fell with Lord Dundee, at the Pass of Killiecrankie. From this time, young Stewart was taught to become the inveterate foe of every red-coat; and this hatred, once instilled, was cherished to the last. He soon became passionately fond of the broad-sword, and excelling his compeers in its exercise, longed for an opportunity of signalizing his valour. This did not occur till 1715, when the Earl of Mar led, or rather misled, some 12,000 Highlanders to the fight at Sheriff-muir. Stewart was among them, burning for fame and vengeance on account of the death of his father. He knew every corner of the country in the district, from his having been shepherd for several years on different farms situated on both sides of the Allan. On this account he was known to "auld Balhaldie," who, having happened to fall in with him the evening previous to the battle, remarked to him, that he (Stewart) being a stout fellow, might be singled out in the approaching conflict, and therefore recommended him to "put a horse-shoe in the crown of his bonnet," which being attended to, was the means of saving his life, as shall be afterwards shown.

The eventful morning arrived, and the Highland army moved from the Moor of Kinbuck to the scene of action. The march, in order that they might obtain possession of the heights before Argyll, was rapid, and proved successful. Mar's lines were hardly formed, before a volley from the "red-coats" brought down a number of Highlanders, and, among the number, the Chief of Clanranald, when the right wing rushed forward with a terrific yell to the onset, with Glengarry at their head. The Highland ranks being rather irregular at the moment of collision with the bayonets of their opponents, and Stewart being a tall stout man, and on the right of the front line, he was instantly singled out by a dragoon, who rode at him full speed, and before Stewart's attention could be directed towards him, a blow from his sabre brought Stewart to his knees; yet, by an effort of strength and agility, he recovered in time to disable and repel his antagonist. Stewart's bonnet having dropt off in the scuffle, he witnessed the happy effects of having paid due regard to Balhaldie's advice, for he found that the horse-shoe had done him good service in warding his sconce from the blow which brought him to his knees, and which the dragoon had so heartily and powerfully dealt, as almost to cut the metal through. Stewart soon refitted his head with the simple yet serviceable head-gear, and joined the mellé of death. He was soon attacked by another dragoon, but this one he saw coming, and was prepared. A single parry and thrust was all that was found necessary to make his assailant drop from his saddle on the earth. A minute or two afterwards, when the whole left wing of the red-coats was on the point of retreat, Stewart observed two or three robust Highlanders, bareheaded, in the centre of the detested red-coats, back to back, dealing death around them. Fearing his hardy countrymen must inevitably be discomfited and slain, with such fearful odds against and around them, he rushed forward with his sword, dirk, and target, and striking to the right and left at the same moment, soon opened his way; and some more Highlanders coming up to their aid, the whole of the scarlet circle was cut to pieces—quarter being neither asked nor given. Thus far, all went well with our hero; but in the pursuit, and near to the farm-house of Stonehill, poor Stewart fell from a musket-shot passing through his thigh. And here he lay until he was fortunately picked up by the victorious wing to which he belonged, on their return to the battle-field in the evening. He shortly afterwards recovered.

Some years after this, Stewart, through the influence of his Jacobitical friends, obtained a lease of the farm already mentioned, and which he continued to hold till his death. At this sequestered muirland spot, several *incog.* meetings of the feudal Chiefs are believed to have been held previous to and during the rebellion of 1745; and here, according to our authority, several arrangements were made with the low country Lairds, friendly to the enterprise. " Auld Calzie," however, was not out himself in this last attempt to restore the exiled Stewarts; but his two eldest sons were in all the engagements, and both died on the Moor of Culloden. From this time, excessive grief for his sons, and disappointment on account of the issue of the enterprise which began so prosperously—together with the news of the dreadful cold-blooded carnage among his countrymen by the Duke of Cumberland, and the disarming act—acted so powerfully upon Calzie's mind, that he fell into an incurable despondency, which gradually impaired his mental faculties, besides wasting his robust frame. Time, however, brought him partially to health of body, but his mind continued imbecile. He survived until 1762, and died at the age of four-score.

We shall add an anecdote of young Rob Roy, in one of his reckless plundering excursions to better his fortune, in which Calzie was concerned, and which happened immediately before the " Forty-five."

A portion of Calzie's black cattle were one morning amissing, and their owner was at last persuaded that they had been *lifted*, although he wondered that the whole, instead of a part, had not been taken. The neighbouring farmers and their shepherds being warned, set off for the different passes to the north to obtain information, while Calzie, who had always his " ain think," took a southward route by Doune. Here meeting with an old acquaintance and kinsman, he informed him of his loss, adding, that all but himself had gone north in pursuit of the *harryers.* " North !" exclaimed his friend, while he buckled on his weapons, " Tat tam scoundrel Rob Oig gaed ower the Brig o' Doune this mornin' wi' a hale drove, an' you may be

sure yours was amang them. He has nae a cloot o' his
ain, an' deil ane will trust him a fardin's worth." There
was not a moment to lose. Calzie, laying his hand on the
basket of his brand, started to his feet, and the two were
mounted and off presently. Rob with his drove were
readily traced by the Fords of Frew to Kippen, and thence
by the high pathway towards Campsie, in the vicinity of
which they were overtaken by their pursuers. After some
merited reproach on Calzie's part towards the young
reiver, he was permitted to select his own cattle from the
rest of the *spulzie*, with which he immediately returned
homewards; but they had gone only a short way back,
when, whom should they meet, riding forward with the
utmost haste and fury, but Calzie's own neighbours, with
others from Strathallan, who at the same time had been
similarly treated, and having got the right scent, were
hastening to the rescue of their cattle from the hands of
the reivers. Redoubling their haste on obtaining additional information, an hour had scarcely elapsed when
they appeared in Calzie's rear with the whole "drove," and
Rob and his four men prisoners. A long consultation was
then held how "young Rob" should be disposed of.
Calzie, "for his father's sake," begged his release, on
promise of amendment. The more furious Strathallan
"lallanders" were for prompt justice at the first tree,
while the more rational and peaceably disposed preferred
committing Rob and his assistants to the care of the
authorities at Stirling. But Rob, "deevil that he was,"
had the policy to bare his breast, and invite some of them
to shoot him on the spot, rather than that he should be
committed to the custody of red-coats. The hated name
"red-coat," old as he was, roused Calzie. He instantly
drew his claymore, and vowed that that should not be
while he lived; and every Highlander present, following
his example, was instantly at his back. The consequence
was, that after a severe reprimand from Calzie, Rob Oig

was permitted to escape; the *irregulars*, who carried scythes, hay-forks, and other such weapons, having lowered their tone for prompt justice, on so sudden an appearance of naked swords and Highland wrath; and the several parties singling out their own cattle from "the drove," departed for their homes, with very little courtesy shewn towards each other.

VII.

YOUNG ROB ROY.

THIS Rob inherited none of the brave and generous characteristics of his father, the far-famed Rob Roy. Destitute of every humane feeling, he was madly, imprudently, heartlessly cruel, and an utter stranger to that cool, calculating courage, and cautious foresight, which distinguished his ancestor in all his exploits. Rushing headlong into every species of crime, and reckless of consequences, it is no wonder that justice should at last have overtaken him, or that the terminating scene of his earthly existence should have, in some measure, been made to atone for the many crimes of which he was certainly guilty.

We shall see, from the following well-authenticated tradition, that at one time young Rob had nearly fallen a victim to his own negligence and want of caution, in one of his forays through the Lowlands:—

Some years before Rob forfeited his life to the violated laws of his country, he, followed by a chosen band of his proscribed clansmen, made a sally from his Highland cave, and suddenly scouring Strathallan, reaped a rich harvest of booty. Upon "pain of death," also, extorting sums of money, he, as will be seen from the sequel, was at this time pretty successful. As fate would have it, however, Rob, feeling not contented with the plunder which had been acquired betwixt Ardoch and Kinbuck, despatched part of "his men," with the Strathallan spoil, home to those seqestered recesses of his almost unapproachable haunts, where he had long eluded the vigilance of those who vainly endeavoured to effect his apprehension,—while at the same time he determined to make a *finale* by plundering some of the Sheriff-muir tenants, who, he knew, had lately before entered into a league to defend themselves "against Rob Oig and all other Highland thieves." Ascending the muir from Kinbuck, with a few of his followers, they soon arrived at the farm-house at Park of Jerah. The doors, in those times always bolted at nightfall, were instantly forced, and the inmates, consisting of Mrs. Monteath and family, summarily ejected at the sword's-point. Monteath himself had been that day at Stirling, and had not returned, but his wife and children expecting him every moment, proceeded on the way by which they knew he would approach. At "Maggy o' the Bog's," about half a mile from her own house, Mrs. Monteith met her husband, fortunately accompanied by " the auld smith o' Keir, a man of uncommon courage and great muscular strength. On learning of this outrage against him, Monteath, with his friend, instantly set about concerting a plan, embracing nothing short of destroying the whole party of plunderers. Knowing something of Rob's extreme negligence and imprudence in conducting his forays, it struck them as likely that he would omit placing sentinels about the house to give alarm. They therefore in that case determined to "rack the door," and then burn the house about the robbers' ears, allowing, if possible, none to escape. On cautiously approaching, they found matters exactly as they supposed. The first sentence that saluted their ears from the interior of the domicile, was from Rob himself, exclaiming, " D—n old Park, we'll no lea'e him a cock to craw "—(an oath, by the bye, from his father's catalogue)—which was responded to by "his men" with a

shout of laughter, while busying themselves in the ransack.
In the hurry and confusion the plunderers, who are said
to have been half-drunk, seem never to have dreamt what
measures were preparing against them. The door was no
sooner fastened than, through the active exertions of Mrs.
Monteath, the neighbouring pendiclers (and they were
then numerous) were alarmed, armed, and in motion, to
annihilate the "common enemy." A hay-rick was just
removed from its site in the barn-yard to the house, to
begin the conflagration, when a dozen, armed with muskets
and swords, appeared at the premises. On observing the
arrival of this formidable party, Monteath, anxious to save
his house and property, proposed that an attempt should
first be made to shoot the robbers through the *bunkers*.
A shot was accordingly fired through one of these *boles*,
and a M'Gregor fell. The whole now rushed to the door,
and finding it fast, were all consternation. Half-a-dozen
bullets at that moment penetrating the wooden boards, and
wounding several of the marauders, heightened their confusion and dismay. At last, after some more firing, Rob
himself called out, begging to be permitted to depart,
farther *unscathed*, upon paying down a sum of money.
Terms agreed on, "Young Rob" tossed out a purse con-
taining "a hunder an' fifty guineas o' gowd;" and the
posse of robbers were permitted to depart one by one,
"through the muckle bunker o' the spence," leaving their
arms behind. Several of the swords of those M'Gregors
were in possession of Monteath's successors at Park,
in 1784.

VIII.

ANECDOTES.

I.—BATTLE OF FALKIRK.

THE following anecdote has been told of a Highland Piper, who was so fortunate, after the above action, as to be enabled to help himself pretty liberally with several articles of value from the pockets and fobs of some fallen Englishmen. Among the articles were two watches, the one gold and the other silver. Holding one in each hand he strutted along till he met a young fellow of a Lowlander, whom he thus addressed :—" My praw laat, ye'll pe puy ta ponny things—she'll gie her ta prass ane for twal, an' ta siller ane for fyfteen *skillin-sassanach.*" The young man exhibited so much alacrity in drawing from a secret corner of his habiliments the sum required, which he immediately handed to the piper, that the latter began to suspect he was dealing with a knowing fellow, and about to part with his " ponny thing " for a sum much below its value. This was grievous, but still more so to part with the money, which, according to the natural course of things with Donald, was no sooner into his hands than it found its way into the secure folds of his ample *Sporran Mollach.* Accordingly, instead of placing either of the watches into the hand which was outstretched to receive one of them—to the dismay of the Lowlander, he saw both put into the purse along with the money. After a few seconds spent in a reverie of dead musing, the piper turned round to his new acquaintance, and said, "My dainty chiel, ye'll pe wantin' ta ponny thing, but bide awee, we'll first tak ta spring on ta pargain, an' part goot frien's ;" and immediately putting his drones in order, he struck up some of his clamorous music. When he had played as long and loud as any but Highland ears could well endure, he cast a stormy glance at the fellow, saying,

"Noo, wad you pe kennin ta name o' ta spring?" "No," responded the unsuspecting man. "No," rejoined Donald, "then she'll pe play 't owre again," and instantly gave vent to the war-notes of *Donald Dhu*, with a vehemence and aspect of countenance that threatened an approaching storm of Highland wrath. Stopping abruptly, he cast a fiery glance at the countryman, saying, "Ye surely pe ken ta spring noo?" "No," was again the reply. "Then," said, Donald, gathering himself up, "her nainsel maun shust pe tell you what ta tune pe say,"—and suiting the action to the word, with his hand upon the basket of his sword, he roared out, "You tam colt, ta tune pe said you paid ta piper wi' ta siller, an' if ye'll no pe awa' as fast as ye can rin, she'll pe stappin her claymore in ye."

II.—BATTLE OF GLADSMUIR.

On the evening of that day on which "Johnny Cope" was so signally and disgracefully defeated at Preston, a number of prisoners, taken in the action, were, for lack of better accommodation, huddled into the barn of a neighbouring farm-yard, over whom was placed a small guard of well-armed Highlanders. Some of the English redcoats, notwithstanding that their situation was every thing but comfortable, could not resist relating jokes to each other, in no very measured undertones, far from being flattering to the soldierly appearance of the northern conquerors. This sport was anything but relished by such of the guard as had caught so much of the English tongue as to understand what was going on at their expense. One mountaineer, of the clan M'Donald, brandishing his sword, and assuming a countenance expressive of contempt, reddened with rage—and making a pause at the barn-door, whence some unhallowed words had just saluted his ear, addressed the group in the following terms :—" Ye ocht to pe respeckin' yer petters—tem tat pe ta real sojars—ye tirty cooarts! Tare no pe ane amang ye a', tat was pe killed tis plessit mornin', but was stickit whaur its no pe decent till say." Taking then a short turn to cool his rage, he resumed his station at the door, and taking a side view of the prisoners, exclaimed—"Wha pe mak' ta *King* put ta *Sojar*—an' wha can pe mak' ta *true* sojar put ta Macdonnell?" A general burst of laughter instantly issued from the barn at the interrogator's clannish ideas, when a voice from the crowd called out—"And who made the MacDonald?" With an air of contemptuous indignation he replied—"Ta Macdonnell *made hersel*—ye tam Shordy's b—h !!"

III.—"DUKE WILLIAM AND A HIGHLANDER."

When the Duke of Cumberland was marching at the head of his horse by the foot of a hill, which lay in his route to Culloden, an ancient Highlander, whose head was silvered by the hand of time, and whose brow was furrowed deep with the toils of former years, meanly dressed in the costume of his country, and mounted on a diminutive shelty, descended from the height, and trotted alongside of the military procession. A lusty dragoon, mounted on a stately English charger, conceiving the poor antiquated mountaineer a subject with which he might make a little sport, seized the old Celt by the collar, lifted him from his *sunks* on the pony, and placed him on the ground, observing that such as he ought to walk on foot, when he travelled with his betters.

Donald, not relishing such treatment, soon found his way to the Duke, and, with bonnet in hand, thus addressed his Grace:—"May it pe pleasin your Grace,— ane o' your Grace's mans hae peen insult her nainsel, an' she'll pe comin' to pe crave ta shatisfactions." "What satisfaction do you want?" interrogated the Duke. "Och, shust ta shatisfactions of ta shentlemans," replied Donald.

"Do you wish to fight him?" continued the Duke. "Ugh, ay—shust fecht her," quoth Donald. "Well, my good old fellow," said the Duke, "if I find you have cause of complaint, you shall have the satisfaction you demand;" and having so said, immediately called a halt, and ordered Donald to point out his man. Donald, in obeisance, turned up his hand to his weather-beaten bonnet, and turning round, soon darted his eye on the object of his resentment. "This old man," said the Duke to the lusty horseman, "complains that you have insulted him. What have you done?" The soldier told him. "Well," resumed the Duke, "I have promised him satisfaction—you must fight him." "That I will, please your Grace," said the bold dragoon, with a sneer of contempt towards Donald. The Duke, turning round to the courageous old Gael, observed to him that he had no sword. "Och, but your Grace's mans hae tae plenty swort—your Grace hae ta cootness to pit her gie ta swort to her nainsel shust a wee while." A sword was ordered immediately, and the necessary arrangements made for deadly conflict. But Donald had seen too many snows to trust his life to a blade of untried metal. He minutely examined the handle, the edge, the point, and the *spring;* and, finally, turning aside to a pool of water, and applying the flat side of the blade to its surface, with one smart stroke broke it in two. After repeated trials with similar effect, the wary old Highlander at last found a blade on which he thought he could depend. This was a friend in need—he kissed the instrument of death, and pressed it to his bosom muttering —"You pe ta true swort—you'll pe her nainsel's pest frient this plessit day." The combatants at last took their ground. The dragoon attacked with fury—sprang, cut, and thrust, but in vain. Donald parried every blow with admirable coolness, and latterly watching his opportunity, with one dexterous cut, laid his antagonist lifeless at his feet; then, turning to the Duke with a smile, said—"tat pe ta way her nainsel's Sheneral, learn her to cut when she wad pe in Shermany;—no like your Grace's mans— aye hack, hackin', an' cut, cuttin'—she shust pe sneck aff ta head at ance."

THE OLD KILBRIDE CASTLE.

Legendary Tales.

I.

THE BLACK KNIGHT OF KILBRYDE.

The Castle of Kilbryde, near Dunblane, said to have been founded by "Sir John of the Bright Sword,"* A.D. 1460, and now a family-seat of Sir James Campbell of Aberuchill, Bart., is very romantically situated. Amid the dusky foliage of lofty planes, that for centuries have braved the angriest storms of winter, and on the very brow of a deep and rugged glen, ornamented with a profusion of natural shrubbery, woodbine, and wild flowers, this interesting specimen of ancient Scottish masonry rises in gloomy and majestic pride. In the dark ages of ignorance, feudal warfare, and superstition, the scenery about this castle was too wildly picturesque not to have had attached to its grottos, ravines, and dark recesses a *quant. suff.* of every variety of those superstitious bugbears of the imagination, which the vulgar of those times conceived to be inseparably associated with every idea of danger, bloody conflict, and sublimity of scene. We are enabled accordingly to discover vestiges of the legends prevalent here in former ages from still existing remnants of ancient oral tale, which are averred to have been handed down, by those who relate them, from a remote period, through a long genealogy of resident progenitors.

---

* Sir John Graham of Kilbryde—"who from his bravery was so called." The "Lands of Kilbryde" were finally ceded to him by his father, Malise, Earl of Menteith, April 7, 1464. The original Charter is still in existence.

Here, we are told by those hoary oracles, that in ancient times, when a warlike chieftain of the Graham family of Kilbryde was soon to fall in feudal strife, or in the service of his country, his bloody apparition might be previously seen at "twilight grey," stalking amongst the loosely-hanging cliffs, or partially discovering its steel-vizored aspect from the hollow crevices of the rifted rocks of Kilbryde Glen; while the long galleries of the castle mournfully resounded to the deep wailings of guardian spirits, foretelling the unavoidable and approaching event. Several instances of such occurrences are enumerated by our local oral authorities, but the particulars are lost, and on such a sublime subject we dare adventure nothing of our own. We select the following from a variety of oral fragments, of which we have obtained a jotting, connected with this ancient barony, as not unworthy of preservation :

Cromlix Castle, of which there are at this day vestiges sufficient to enable us to appreciate its original grandeur—although it is said never to have been finished—stood within a few miles of the Castle of Kilbryde. The Barony of Cromlix was of considerable extent, and was long the paternal estate of a very ancient and honourable family of the name of Chisholm. With a Sir Malise Graham, called "The Black Knight of Kilbryde," a young lady of the Cromlix family fell deeply in love; and the ruthless Knight taking advantage of the violent passion this lady entertained for his person, clandestinely decoyed her from her "father's ha'," seduced, and afterwards basely murdered her. Her disconsolate parents consulted every second-sighted seer and astrologer in the country to no purpose—although the Black Knight should alone have been applied to, as he only could have solved the mystery. It was latterly rumoured that Kilbryde Castle was haunted by a *ghaist*, and that it had been seen of different persons, *arrayed in the white robes of death, sullied with blood*—and last of all, it was promulgated that the Black Knight had been slain in battle, where, dying in great agony, the last word he was heard to utter was the name *Chisholm*. But the death of her seducer and murderer did not appease the manes of the murdered lady. The ghost appeared frequently, and for some time afterwards, to different inmates of Kilbryde Castle, beckoning those to approach with whom *it* seemed anxious to confer, although no one of the menials appears to have had nerve sufficient to risk a midnight rencontre with a spirit not of this world. It was reserved to the resolute courage of a succeeding Knight, to set the matter at rest. He had been heard to declare, that should this *wraith* be a "goblin damned," or a messenger from the lower regions of the universe, he should like, from a personal interview, to know why it so cowardly and dastardly, under shade of night, dared to annoy his servants and vassals, and did not venture to accost himself. It was not long after that he obtained a gratification of his presumptuous and, considering the general belief of the times, rashly-expressed wish. The Knight, however, was brave, and "fair play cared na de'ils a bodle." One dark evening, at a late hour, the ghost saluted him at his own garden gate, and signified to him he should follow. With some hesitation he did so, through the rustling underwood to the glen below, where the spot was shewn at which his predecessor had perpretrated the unhallowed deed, and buried the bloody corpse. Here the "departed shade" of the once beautiful Lady Ann enjoined the Knight, as he valued his own repose, and that of the *spirit* that addressed him, to the performance of certain things which were divulged to him. And most faithfully did he acquit himself of his engagements. The mortal remains of the murdered lady were removed, and received christian burial—the troubled ghost retired to the shades of its ancestors—and the melancholy story was thenceforth caught hold of by the bards and minstrels of Kilbryde, the foregoing fragment of which has been recovered from the recital of a genuine oralist, after a lapse of many generations.

II.

THE WITCHES O' LOGIE.

ABOUT the eighteenth or twentieth year of last century, the " Witches o' Logie " having then arrived at the climacteric of their repute, their "auld daddy, the De'il," in *propria persona*, occasionally presided at and superintended their midnight revels. Here, as at Alloway Kirk, "the Auld Chiel" is said to have generally assumed the canine shape, but invariably appeared in a different character. Instead of being a *Piper*, as in Ayrshire, he condescended, from the superior reputation which " his Witches o' Logie " had acquired in gaining proselytes, to be to them a more menial source of amusement; he was taper-bearer, and his blue torch being socketed *a posteriori*, his skippings and boundings about the " Warlock Knowe," and the grand rendezvous at " Carly Craig," were celebrated as having afforded infinite amusement to the merry devils who gambolled around him. Repeatedly, it is said, the then minister of Logie was annoyed by this " august personage," in the shape of a large shaggy dog, jet black, " wi' awfu' lang teeth an' red een; and," it is added, "the minister kent him by his *cloots* (hoofs), which, it would seem, as is believed at this day by some, he cannot metamorphose. The " Witches o' Logie " had various out-post stations in the neighbourhood of Logie. Those at " Parson Leys " and " Jerah Glen " were most dreaded by the credulous. " Clooty " sometimes visited these posts in different shapes. He was familiarly known at Parson Leys by the appellation of " Auld Roughy," and at Jerah he was called " Auld Donald," from his having here assumed the human shape in the garb of a Highlander, and was always known from his cloven feet. In the dark, deep, narrow, and precipitous Glen of Jerah, shepherds used to tell how they had witnessed " Auld Donald " suspending himself from unapproachable and dreadful precipices, in order, as they suspected, to decoy them to destruction, while obeying the dictates of humanity in endeavouring to get at and " cut him down." The out-post witches were scarcely less dreaded. The " Auld wife o' Jerah " becoming unwell, declared she was *witched* by " Auld Meg o' Ashintrool " and " Black Kate o' Parson-lees," but the good man took his gun, charged it with a silver button, and compelled them to undo the incantation. " Auld Lizzy Monteath o' Park " was similarly affected—had a " bairn like a ghaist," —and all was ascribed to witchcraft, " ill-een," and " Auld Donald o' Jerah."

Our narrative would indeed be interminable were we to notice half of the legends still current of the " Evil Ane," and the " Witches o' Logie." We shall therefore close with a short story, well authenticated, and which, perhaps, is not unworthy of preservation," as illustrative of the superstitious absurdities prevalent about a century ago in the parish of Logie.

A worthy member of the session of Logie, returning home one dusky evening from a shooting excursion, with a well charged musket, which he had some years before picked up on the heights of Sheriff-muir, some days after the battle, thought he perceived the devil on a jutting fragment of the " Carly Craig," and in the very shape so currently ascribed to him at the time by the gossips of the parish of Logie. This man might, perhaps, be somewhat more superstitious than some of his brethren of the present day, but it will be allowed he was equally courageous. He no sooner beheld the foul thief than he resolved on having a shot at him. To ensure effect, while he kept a fixed eye on the supposed devil, he slipped a small silver coin into his gun, and, although his hair was on end, after ejaculating a short prayer, he kneeled down, and proceeded cautiously to take deliberate aim. At last he drew the trigger—when off went the shot, and down fell the devil, "heels-o'er-head," with a hideous moan, to the bottom of the rugged and precipitous rock. The good man lost not a moment in communicating this gratifying intelligence to his minister; and accordingly rushed into the reverend presence, with his gun in his hand, exclaiming, "the de'il's dead noo, the de'il's dead noo, Sir—there's the gun that did the deed." As soon as morning dawned, the reverend gentleman and his elder hurried to the spot, to ascertain whether his Satanic majesty had forgot anything in the shape of a carcase in his hurry the previous night; but to the no little chagrin and perplexity of both they discovered that instead of "a great black dog wi' lang teeth" the body of a beautiful pet goat, the property of a poor woman, grazing among the cliffs, had been mistaken for "the de'il," by the unerring eye of the zealous elder of Logie.

The story adds, and it is often told, that the minister on the following Sunday took occasion to allude to the affair from the pulpit, when he made a digression in a strain which, although it would be considered not a little whimsical and ridiculous in the present day, was by no means rare, or liable to be considered outrageously extravagant a hundred years since. "My friends," he said, "the Evil One may appear in many forms. He may appear like a black collie dog, or he may enter, as of old, into living animals; and, as on a late occasion, he may enter into a harmless goat. Nay, my friends, he may enter into yoursel's, an' gar ye cut yer craigs and hang yersels. Oh, my friends, beware o' this enemy; we are told in this blessed book (laying his hand on the Bible) that he goes about like a roaring lion. He may appear like a *lion*, and why not in *different* shapes. But oh, my friends, dinna think ony earthly gun will shoot the deevil—there is but *ae* gun that will shoot the evil enemy, and that is the gun of the gospel." Then holding up the book in both hands, he added, in the same musical intonation of voice—" This is the gun that will shoot the deevil—the *only* gun that will shoot the deevil. Oh, shoot him then every one of you, wi' *this* gun, and he *shall* be shot."

III.
"DOCTOR URE."

" Doctor Ure," the *hero* of these traditional gleanings, was at the climacteric of his reputation about the middle of last century, and flourished with increasing celebrity from 1700 till about that time. His usual residence was for many years at a little *coterie*, on the banks of the Endrick, a few miles distant from the village of Kippen, where he was consulted by multitudes of the superstitious and credulous, on the subjects of witchcraft, ghosts, incantations, and other bugbears of the current belief then prevalent in the country. This personage, from his own natural cunning and sagacity, it would appear, had become invested by the vulgar with many and various supernatural attributes. He had nostrums for all diseases, and salves for all sores. Possessed of a secret charm against the power of witchcraft, he was consulted on that score much to his own private emolument; and as a conjurer of *ghaists* he was unrivalled. But, "in the second sight, he was without a peer" then living. Whatever were the catastrophes which had befallen poor benighted mortals—whether amid the "whirling drift" of the wintry storm, or the violence of the raging torrent—whether from the spiteful delusions of the water-kelpy at "midnight murk," by the swampy lake, or the deceitful lantern of " Dank Will," sporting where " Danger throws him down to sleep," amongst frightful precipices, over deep *linns*—

Dr. Ure, by simply revolving his eye-balls upwards in their sockets, was believed to *see* the circumstances precisely as they occurred, depicted in rapid succession on a certain interior membrane of his *caput*, and that in consequence he was enabled to inform the consulting applicants at what place the " lifeless corse " of their deceased friend would be found. The prophetic gift, with which he was regarded as being endowed, was similarly remarkable—future calamities to individuals being predicted, on application, exactly in the same ocular way. Of this Doctor's detection of the pranks o' witches—of his infallible charms against witchcraft, of his manifold predictions, of the ghosts, water-wraiths, bogles, and *devils*, which he had conjured and *laid*, we have innumerable oral relations handed down to us at the present time. Let the following suffice as a specimen :—

The Barony of Kilbryde, in Western Perthshire, one hundred years ago, was, it would appear, not less fertile in the produce of warlocks and their malignant helpmates, than the district of Torryburn ; and the *daylight*, with which the worthies of the former had been then favoured, in matters of witchcraft and fairy superstition, seems to have been not a whit less brilliant than that which illuminated the *sensorium* of the Rev. Allan Logan of the latter—to say nothing of Mass Robert Kirke of Aberfoyle, whose skill in divining the mysteries of Fairyland had created a wonderful sensation in that countryside some years previously. The chapel burying ground of Kilbryde was, in those days, famed as a favourite resort of " hornie and his witches ;" also a knoll in the vicinity, that of the Fairy-Queen and her green-coated pigmies. The fairies, it would appear, were here more dreaded than even the de'il with his hags mounted on their broomsticks, and all their seething cauldrons ; they being permitted, it was supposed, to kidnap the tithe of unchristened children from their mothers' sides while they slept, replacing them with their own "unearthly skin-an'-bane gorbels;" whereas the witches' pranks were confined to "drawin' the tether," and now and then inflicting a mishap on individuals obnoxious to them and their cantrips, or invoking the wrath of the elements upon those who treated them unkindly, or neglected to deprecate their vengeance.

At Bridge-hill of Kilbryde, in those days, dwelt a solitary pedlar of the name of Scobie, who, it was said, earned his livelihood by trucking with the fairies. Nobody knew where he disposed of his merchandise; and the coin, of which he was always plentifully possessed, was strange, and the legends impressed upon it so "awfu'" and mysterious, that it was believed to be no other than the coin of Elfland, whence it was averred it must have been procured. This person at last went amissing. He had been one evening in a neighbouring farm-house with his pack, when he appeared "fay-like." This neighbour, in whose house he is said to have passed the evening, accompanied him so far on the way home. On parting, some unusual and remarkable noises were heard, upon which the pedlar was invited to return, but he "would not be advised," and went on. Next morning it was ascertained the pedlar had not gone home, and immediately the whole Barony concluded he must have been carried off by his customers, the fairies, "pack and all." A near relative of "the lost wight," residing in Dunblane, having felt an interest, at least in the *pack*, went off to "Dr. Ure, the warlock," to consult him on the matter—he being possessed of every *sight* in all such mysteries. The Doctor appeared in his leather breeks, green-sleeved coat, and red night-cap," with his "witch-book an' black-art stick in his hand." The known circumstances of the disappearance of the packman—his habits and his character being narrated—we are told that the "white o' the warlock's een turned up" for a considerable time, during which he shook repeatedly "like the aspen leaf," and appeared convulsed with terror. On recovering, he shook his head and said, in a piteous tone—" Aye, he *is* awa' wi' the fairies—I saw the knowe openin', an' *them* drawin' him in. They'll birze his puddin's out, steal a' his guids, and then spue him out. Seek! seek! seek!" the seer exclaimed, "and ye'll find his corpse in a little glen within sight o' the Chapel o' Kilbryde." It is but justice to add that, although many little glens were long sought in vain for Scobie's body, he was found dead in a little glen, some months afterwards, which is called *Scobie's Wood* at this day.

A hypochondriac shoemaker, who resided at Muir-mill, on the banks of the Carron, and who had been long haunted by an apparition, was advised to consult Dr. Ure, in order to have the demon conjured and allayed. The *ghaist*, he said, haunted him night and day, sleeping and awake; he could not put a *steek* in a shoe, nor *rozet* a *lingle*, but it sat opposite his stall, mimicking and mocking him, and that he "wasna feared for't neither." He had tried, he added, to banish it from his presence by throwing awls, size-sticks, and even his stall itself, at the *being's* head; but the whole, it seems, passed through the shadowy form, like the weapon of Fingal through the spirit of Loda. "Aye! aye!" quoth the warlock, on learning the *symptoms*—then "whumlin' round his een in his head," he took a peep into the interior, and afterwards commenced divination by his book and staff. "Isna yer ghaist like a rickle o' banes rowed up in an auld din hide?" interrogated the Doctor. "Aye," replied the dealer in leather, "I see't this moment —the blue lowe comes out o' its mouth, and the red fire from its e'e-holes." The Doctor then caused the poor shoemaker to strip to the skin, when, producing a box of enchanted salve, he liberally besmeared the back of his patient with the ointment. Shortly afterwards he fell into a profound sleep, no doubt from the narcotic effects of the unction which had been used. What were the Doctor's proceedings while he slept he could not tell; but on awaking, the warlock showed him the identical *ghaist* by which he had been so much troubled, "rowed up in an auld hide," in a corner. "There's the ghaist," quoth the Doctor, "it'll fash ye nae mair—gae awa' hame, and be sure ye *throw yere breeks ower your shouther* gaun through the muir, an look na behind you a' the gate hame." The shoemaker, obeying the seer's injunctions, was never more troubled with the apparition.

From this and many other anecdotes it is evident that the Doctor, as he was universally styled in the country, owed not a little of his magical celebrity to his having possessed a more than ordinary share of shrewdness, and, what was of no less essential importance to him in the character which he had assumed, a deep acquaintance with human nature—and that thus he was accustomed to view matters with the eye of a philosopher, although he found it more convenient to indulge his countrymen in attributing all his skill and lore to second sight and supernatural gifts.

Dr. Ure was consulted on less serious occasions, in those times of ignorance and credulity. One time the *kye* of Cullings took such a *rowtin* that their proprietor and others averred that they must have been *witched*. Night and day, says our oralist, for a whole week the braes of Cromlix had re-echoed to the unremitted bellowings of the byres, when it was resolved to send for Dr. Ure, the warlock, to divine the matter. The Doctor, after casting his cantrips and scrutinizing his *caput*, as usual, declared it was *ill-een*; then touching each animal with his magic-staff, he ordered them all to be unloosed and driven to the top of Slimmaback (a hill in the vicinity) and back again, at a hard trot, by which time, he foretold, the *rowtin* would leave them. Accordingly this was done, which had the effect of blowing off their *orrow* wind before their return.

For the *black-leg* in cattle, Dr. Ure is said to have had

an infallible specific, which procured him great fame. His mode of averting the contagion of that disease, however, savoured so much of Druidical barbarism, that we wonder this certainly sagacious old carle could think of recommending it; but he, perhaps, really believed in its *efficacy* himself, as well as others who have been known to try it, within these few years, not ten miles north of Stirling. By way of propitiating the *Powers of the air*, who were believed to have all these matters confided to them, the Doctor caused a young and uninfected heifer to be buried alive; then, to *seal* the matter, he used his incantations around the hole where the brute was just immolated.

It were endless to recount the various prodigies of Dr. Ure. He had nostrums for all diseases, and a *cure* for every thing. Against inconstancy, in either husband or wife, his specifics were frequently applied for; and for the "haggard fiend jealousy," his incantations were deemed the *ne plus ultra*. He commanded the affections of maidens, and controlled or alienated those of young men. He was accounted superior to every familiar spirit, and to have been empowered by the Deity to check the pranks of Satan, and all his tribes of imps, goblins, witches, fairies, *ghaists*, and other bugbears—for which purpose he had been endowed with second-sight, and other super-human faculties. In short Dr. Ure was one of those sagacious mortals who profited by the foolish credulity of the vulgar of the times in which he lived.

IV.

THE LAIRD O' ARGATY.

At a period, not very remote, when the extirpation of witches was zealously prosecuted by the laity of Scotland, many were condemned by the superstitious notions of the times, and the rigid persecuting ignorance and weak credulity of the clergy, to perish in the flames.

In those times, says tradition, there lived at Blenboard, near the Mill of Kilbryde, a *trio* of miserables, whose imaginations were perpetually haunted with the dreadful idea that one day or other they should be seized by the local authorities, and burnt at the stake, for the *crime* of witchcraft. This dreadful doom, they augured, would befal them from a consciousness of the oddly-marked peculiarities of their own features, and the unearthly and forbidding dis-symmetry of their persons. So far, indeed, according to our story, were those frightful forebodings carried by those gloomy eccentrics, that their intellects became latterly impaired, and thus, doubtless, the fate which they had so long dreaded was hurried on by their own distracted terrors. So far as we can judge from the description given of the corporeal conformation of the frame-work of those beings, it may be safely questioned whether, properly speaking, they could *possibly* be possessed of intellects. Their names were *Willie, Robin,* and *Mall,* brothers and sister. They were possessed of vast wealth, which they inherited from their progenitors, but which they kept concealed, living most miserably; and being perpetually covered with filth, and enveloped in rags, their appearance must have been most grotesque and hideous. Willie is described as being beardless and bluff-visaged, with prominent rosy cheeks, large hook-nose, and small dark deeply-sunk eyes. Immediately above the latter the forehead receded, where it was instantly lost in masses of red bristly hair. His arms were short and thick, his shoulders high, and his neck long—the trunk of his body thick and round—and, withal, he was mounted on a pair of disproportionately-long " knull-kneed " limbs. Robin, on the contrary, was a shrivelled diminutive being, with a *scranky* and concave countenance, flat nose, wide mouth, and long tapering chin, stuck thickly with black bristles. His eyes were deep and hollow, and the eyebrows shaggy. His " biped-end " was bandy, irregular,

and crooked, and his feet large and flat. Mall was the
very counterpart of Robin—only the *whisker* about her
mouth and chin was somewhat more inclined to *white*,
being less *rank*, more thinly sown, and curly. Such is the
description of the " twa warlocks of Blenboard " and their
sister, " the witch," given by a fire-side oralist still alive,
who verily believes in the authenticity of her relation,
which, she says, she had from her grandmother seventy
years ago—and who actually witnessed the burning of
those beings about a mile from the Chapel of Kilbryde,
and " a' for witchin' the Laird o' Argaty."

Some more particulars are related by the same old
woman, probable enough, and which may be really true.
Among these we may mention the following:—The old
Castle of Argaty, the ruins of which might be traced in
1800, was not far distant from the secluded domicile of
the devoted subjects of our story. It is said the Laird
o' Argaty coveted their wealth, which, added to the probability of his verily believing what few in those days
would think of doubting, on rational motives, namely,
that the wretched brothers and sister held communion
with the powers of darkness, it is very probable that he
soothed his conscience and gratified his avarice at the
same time, in raising the hue and cry against his neighbours. At all events, our oralist relates, that resolved to
have possession of their riches, he feigned sickness, and
denouncing the miserable trio as having agency with Satan,
declared that his illness arose from their incantations.
They were accordingly apprehended, and, as generally
happened in the period of barbarous ignorance to which
we refer, their wretched garbs and deformed persons
afforded ample corroboration of the equally well-founded
evidence which was brought against them at their trial.
It is almost unnecessary to add that they were convicted,
and, as our aged oralist relates, immediately afterwards
burnt at the " Rowan Stock of Kilbryde."

V.

THE WARLOCK O' DUNBLANE.

WATTY BRYCE, the hero of this authentic tale, is believed to have *flourished* as an *uncanny* wight among the citizens of Dunblane, in the days of our Scottish Solomon, King James the *Last*. It is well known that at the nod of this sapient monarch, and by means of his antiwitchery publication, myriads of "witches and warlocks" were conjured up, to the great terror and alarm of the newly-converted presbyterians, and their superstitious spiritual pastors. In those days, from writings still extant, as well as from gleanings from oral tradition, Dunblane seems to have been abundantly favoured with that spirit of illumination which so happily distinguished its august monarch from every other potentate on the face of the earth, since the days of his great prototype, the Son of David—although for a long time "the maist pairt of ye inhabitants in ys town and nither pairts about had stuid over in sic fear, yt they never durst accuse" our hero, Watty Bryce. But as time wore on, and Adam Ballenden in 1615 obtained the Bishopric—"ye heall toun and sundrie gentillmen yrabout" seem to have conceived that the new Bishop would listen most religiously to "ye strange dittayes" which they now had the courage to prefer against Watty. For we find the Bishop (Maie 13, 1615), in consequence of an application from Dunblane, numerously subscribed, in a letter from SCONE, applying for a "Commissione" to "ye Laird of Keir, Sir Geo. Muschat of Burnbanke, Knyght, James Kinross of Kippenross and to William Blakwoode and Jhon Morrisone, Bailyies of Dunblane, for putting ys man to inquest," he being one "yt haid dune grett mischief be his sorceries and witchcraft." His Lordship's letter, "desyrand ye comissione," had, it appears, been duly attended to by "yt worthie minister, the Rev. Jhon Rollok" of Edinburgh, to whom it was addressed—this divine having lost not a moment in applying to the *Secret Council*, procuring the document and transmitting it to Dunblane. In virtue of this, poor Watty Bryce was in a very short time "fast in bandis." His hoary locks and wrinkled features, instead of exciting commiseration, had only the effect of furnishing his superstitious persecutors with additional reasons why "ys boundis sud be purgit of ye pestilent fellow." The *Evil-ane* was observed by those who apprehended him, girnin' in his very face—while the onlookers with what was called *holy fear*, blessed themselves that "the devil durst gang nae farer than the tether wad lat him"—to say nothing of those who had *delated* the old man as a *warlock*, and who gazed on the intended victim with tremulous apprehension, while they no doubt considered how they "wald give yair conscience upon the gritt damage yai had sustenit be his cantrips."

When the Commissioners met within "ye tolbuith" of Dunblane to hold the inquest, the Laird of Keir proposed (contrary it seems to the then usual practice in such cases) that the prisoner should be present to confront his accusers—and that he should be permitted to exculpate himself by cross-questioning the witnesses—in which proposition he was supported by the Laird of Kippenross and the Knyght of Burnbanke. The Bailies, however, opposed this with all the sturdy pith and fury which so much distinguished the bigotry and superstitious ignorance of the times. They averred that none of his accusers would venture to tell the truth face to face with this evil enemy of all good; but Kippenross frankly avowed his determination to sift the matter fairly, and had the hardiness and firmness even to drop such contemptuous hints against the whole proceedings as shewed he was no believer in their absurdities. In this he was supported by Keir, who failed not to tell them that the Bishop himself was of the same mind. Nor was this all. He even went so far as to propose the propriety and justice of burning the accuser, and setting the poor old prisoner at liberty.

"Beilzie Morisone" stood aghast on hearing this, but on recovering from his trepidation, he solemnly reminded them what they were about—"that the *great King James* was a true believer in witches—nay, that *the great and ever blessed John Knox* himself was a believer in the existence of witches, and that every godly minister of the true Reformed Kirk of Scotland at that day believed in the Bible and in *witches.*"

Scepticism in the creed of the worthy authorities, both royal and reverend, referred to by the sapient Bailie, was no longer minced. The Laird of Keir pitied the credulity and ignorance of those who recognised such absurdities as part of their faith. Kippenross contemptuously observed that the ministers of the *True Kirk*, as it was called, were, with few exceptions, grossly illiterate and ignorant—so much so, that he had lately heard one of them from the pulpit aver that the natural phenomena of Solar Eclipses were nothing else than miracles performed by the direct interposition of heaven, that poor benighted Scotland might profit thereby. The Knyght bore testimony to the excellent character of the prisoner. He had known him for forty years, and his honest name he trusted would not be sullied by the visionary accusations of folly and ignorance. He had been industrious all his life, and possessed more than ordinary sagacity—and all that could be urged against him was, that the latter property had been more imprudently than wisely exercised, so as to work on the fears of the weak and credulous.

The "Beilyie" here again rose and essayed to speak, with horror depicted in every lineament of his lank countenance. But he had just said that little more than "aughteen zeirs" had elapsed since the last "awfu' and fearfu' Eclipse whilk the Reverend and godly Robert Rollok, moderator of ye General Assemblie, of ye True Kirk of Scotland, and a man of gritt knowledge, and learned in all ye wisdom of ye Egyptians, had tauld from the poupit, was a *fearfu' warning to sinfu' Scotland sent by——*" when he was abruptly interrupted by the three gentlemen, who formed a majority of the inquest, peremptorily ordering the prisoner to the bar, and which order was immediately attended to by the *lictors* in attendance.

Bryce appeared, and with confidence too, for he knew the majority of the tribunal were men whose sense and education had placed them above the superstitious ignorance of the times. Accordingly, he had no sooner approached the bar than he boldly requested and obtained permission to address a few words to their "Honors." From the tale which Watty here told, it would appear that during the three days and nights of his incarceration, he had not been permitted to sleep; that Bailies Blakwoode and Morisone had been during all that time at stated intervals torturing him most cruelly, endeavouring to extort a confession from himself that he was actually a *warlock*, and in compact with the devil. He had been "stabbit wi' swords, dirks, and daggers," by the Bailies' attendants, and sometimes by themselves, in many parts of the body, while bound and unable to do anything for himself. And, committing his cause to the three gentlemen, he craved redress for the barbarous usage he had experienced.

The Knight of Burnbanke fired instantly on learning these particulars, and rising, turned hastily round to his coadjutors, the Bailies, enquiring if the prisoner had stated facts. The Bailies could not contradict what had been said by the old man, but pled common custom, and the necessity of extorting confession by torture, of such heinous and hellish criminals as *warlocks* must necessarily be—the enemies of both God and man. Whereupon the Knight, in the utmost ire, declared that by such means he could make the Bailies themselves confess being in compact with the prince of darkness, or anything else which might be suggested to them—and forthwith proposed to send for Cromlix, hereditary superior of the regality, in order to have his consent to try the experiment. The proposition being warmly acceded to by Keir and Kippenross, the *ruse* was not without its effect; for the two Bailies retired from the bench thunderstruck, and the three gentlemen proceeded to call evidence. But one *witness* only, however, was examined, an old woman named Elspat Whirrit, who said she did not believe Watty Bryce could deny but that he had witched her, seeing he had, thirty years before, appeared to her in a dream, and exhorted her to leave her husband and elope with another man—since which occurrence, having taken his advice, she never had a day to do well; all which she ascribed to Watty's evil counsel in her dream. It is almost needless to add that this was a sufficient specimen of the *evidence* likely to be adduced. In a word, the Court broke up in disgust, and Watty Bryce was discharged. The Bailies, however, reported the matter their own way to the General Assembly—but Cromlix being rather more inclined to Episcopacy than Presbytery, found means to have the Bailies hanged at the " gallow-lee " of Dunblane a short time thereafter. So saith our tale, the greater part of which is founded upon written documents, and corroborated by tradition.

VI.

FAIR QUEEN HELEN.

Some centuries anterior to the era ascribed to the poems of Ossian, and before the invasion of Britain by the Romans, or the formation of Agricola's Camp at Ardoch, tradition states that betwixt Kinbuck-bridge, near Dunblane, and the foot of Gleneagles, a considerable way to the east of the village of Blackford—a distance of twelve or fifteen miles—all that fertile plain, bounded on the north by the Grampians, and on the south by the Ochils, through which the river Allan now winds its still and serpentine course, was one beautiful expanse of water, varying from one mile to three in breadth; and that the numerous tributary streams which now fall into that river, were then discharged at the eastern extremity of this lake, and were conveyed to the Earne by the water of Ruthven, which washes the foot of Craig-rossy, below Auchterarder. Our story continues to inform us that this lake, which was as clear as crystal, and abounded with the finest trout, was a favourite resort of the ancient Caledonian monarchs, and that here a royal fishing-boat was constantly kept in repair.

A Scottish king, but what king is not said, on a pleasure tour to this lake, was accompanied by his queen, whose name is handed down to us as " the Fair Queen Helen," and this queen was accidentally drowned. The version of some says that the accident happened from the pleasure-boat being upset; while that of others, with whom the writer has conversed, describes it as having happened in a different, but more particular and interesting manner. The lake, they say, was fordable for *horses* at the modern hamlet of Blackford; and here, in attempting to get over with some attendants, the queen's horse having gone beyond his depth, she was carried off by the current, enveloped in the deep, and unfortunately lost. The same authorities add that an expression in his own vernacular Celtic, at the time used by the disconsolate monarch of Caledonia, which is understood to mean that it was a *black* ford to *him*—is at this day perpetuated in the name of the village.

The king, refusing to be comforted for the loss of his " Fair Helen," whom he loved tenderly (and who for her numerous virtues was adored by all his people), after a long and fruitless search for the lifeless corpse, determined to have the lake drained for the purpose of recovering it. This being discovered to be practicable, the king, seconded to a man by his dutiful subjects (who were collected in great numbers from all parts of the kingdom, deploring the loss of their beautiful queen), after great labour effected the purpose of completely running off the lake by a deep *cut*, at the place where, about the middle of last century, the bridge of Kinbuck was built. After a long and diligent search by thousands of his Caledonians, the the King had the melancholy pleasure of hearing it announced that the " mortal remains " were at last discovered, but in so mutilated and disfigured a state that they could not be removed. On this account, continues our traditional authority, a vast monumental mound of earth was thrown up over the body of " Fair Queen Helen," which is shewn as such at this day. It is of an oblong or elliptical shape at the base, is of considerable height, and, gently sloping to the top, terminates in a narrow ridge. This ancient mound may be seen, overgrown with broom, about two miles below Blackford, by the river side. It is unquestionably artificial.

It will be difficult for those who are well acquainted with the formation of Strathallan entirely to discredit the above tradition ; this much at least is certain, that in very ancient times it was a lake. The story is yet familiar to every old residenter in and about that Strath, and although the recitals of different old people may vary considerably, they all agree in the following essential particulars :—That the whole Strath was anciently a lake ; that this lake was drained to recover the body of a Scottish queen here accidentally drowned ; that that queen's name was Helen, or " Fair Queen Helen ;" that the mound of earth near Blackford was raised over her body to perpetuate her memory ; and that after the lake was dried, its *site* was named Strath-*Helen*—now, corruptly, Strathallan. It may be remarked by the way, that the earthen mound, from its vicinity to the Camp at Ardoch, and its being nearly a miniature resemblance of the hills at Dunipace, may by many be considered a Roman antiquity, but every variety of our story positively confutes this supposition.

To those who are strangers to the singular situation of this Strath, a few remarks may be necessary to convince them of the plausibility of our ancient oral tale. The whole Strath is almost a *dead* level. Betwixt Blackford and Kinbuck-bridge there is not a fall of above twelve feet. The heights on each side of the Allan at this bridge are high, and are separated only by the breadth of the channel ; and, from actual survey, it has been lately calculated that not a very large sum of money would be necessary to defray the expense of raising such an embankment here as would occasion such a retrocession of the river as to cause it to seek its pristine course by the Ruthven, after forming a lake of the extent handed down by oral tradition. There is no other outlet by which the surplus of water could otherwise issue—the sloping dales of the Grampians on the one side, and those of the Ochils on the other, presenting insurmountable barriers. In a word, although this certainly old tale be not entitled to implicit reliance in many particulars, yet, unlike many legendary fictions, it is so strikingly plausible that it must have been originally founded on *facts*, and is consequently the more worthy of preservation.

Biographical Sketches.

I.

BESSY STEIN.

BESSY STEIN, the subject of this traditional sketch, was born in the vicinity of Craigforth, about the year 1730. Her immediate progenitors were, in their day, deemed respectable, living "soberly, religiously, honestly, and industriously," so far as was known to the Kirk-Sessions of Stirling, as their certificates, extant among "Bessy Stein's remains," yet testify. Her father seceded from "the Kirk" with his pastor, the Rev. Mr Erskine, but his wife preferred adhering to the Establishment, orthodox or heterodox—being, as she said, weary of perpetual jarring and innovation in religious matters. Old Bessy is said to have been a woman of much shrewdness, and of sanctified exterior—but withal of *principles*, as she called them, deeply imbued with a species of quaint hypocrisy and deceit, which, in those days, among the demi-ignorant and fanatical, were readily mistaken for true piety under the vizor which the ingenuity of this female hypocrite enabled her to assume. She was consequently esteemed among the Seceders of Craigforth, as a good godly woman—a woman of great knowledge—and, although "still in the gall of bitterness and bond of iniquity," yet one who, it was fondly hoped, as she would be an ornament to the Secession, would soon be enabled "through the strength of divine grace," to "burst the bands of Satan asunder,"

and to become, like her husband, a disciple of the Truth—
a hope, however, never to be realised, for Old Bessy
remained steadfast in the good old faith—adhering to her
"principles" till the last.

Young Bessy became a genuine twig of the mother-
tree. Old Bessy was her sole preceptor—her father, good
honest man, having "for peace-sake," after a severe struggle,
been obliged to concede this point entirely to his wife.
And from the following anecdote of Young Bessy's pre-
cocity of *talent*, we must admit that her preceptorship
could hardly have fallen into abler hands :—The Reverend
Ebenezer Erskine was on a visit at her father's house, when
Young Bessy had just completed her sixth year. Finding
the girl an adept in answering questions from the Shorter
Catechism, the reverend gentleman took higher ground,
and, after a lecture on matrimony, enquired, amongst
other things, "Where are marriages made up, my little
dear ?" "Ou—just at Fairs, Markets, and *Tent Preachin's*,
as my mither says," replied Young Bessy. "Na, na,
Betsy," said the minister, "marriages are made up in
Heaven." "Yer wrang noo, Sir," smartly responded Young
Bessy, with her eyes glistening, "there's *mony little-worth
marriages* now-a-days, as my mither tells my father—*they*
canna be made up in that guid place." The worthy man
is said to have smiled at Young Bessy's cleverness, while
her mother, who, in contempt of the presence of her
husband's minister, went about her kitchen-work as usual
—ordered the girl peremptorily to the door—little Bessy's
father meanwhile lugubriously silent, staring as if his best
breeches had long been consigned to the custody of his
spouse.

Young Bessy remained with her parents till her twelfth
year, improving in all the accomplishments of her mother.
At this period, matters going hard with her father, she
became servant in a family near Gargunnock, where she
was so much liked, that in a short time she was entrusted

with the sole management about the kitchen and dairy, under her mistress. Here Bessy spent sixteen years of her life. In those days an extensive contraband trade in brandy and *Hollands* was carried on from France and the Netherlands, through the Western Highlands, to the south of Scotland, and Bessy's master, whose farm-steading lay in the southward track of the adventurers, was a willing, useful, and successful abettor of the traffic, receiving in return for his aid and assistance in procuring *merchants* for the *goods*, and betimes, in securing the *kegs* from reprisal, a cask of brandy or gin now and then for his own use from the smugglers. Here, no doubt, during her long sojourn in the family, Bessy Stein was subjected to great temptations. Bad habits are more readily acquired than good, and as "dribbles o' brandy" were frequently in her way, we need not feel astonished that she should not have mustered so much self-denial as resist *the enemy*, in *his* perpetual assaults. Indeed, we are assured, so far was this from being the case, that Bessy's *constitution* and the strong aromatic flavour of *Cogniac* became shortly inseparable—became indeed *incorporated.* Yet, in justice we must at the same time record that instead of obliterating those religious predilections which she had imbibed from her mother, the *moderate* use of strong drink seems to have had the effect of preserving them in all their strength —perhaps somewhat in the manner that *colours* are *burnt* into glass. Bessy, indeed, never partook of the *cordial* but in moderation, although in the latter part of her life, at *brithals, blythe-meats*, and *dredgies*, she is alleged to have ventured a *nick* too deep, from her ignorance of the adulterated qualities of the liquors produced, as also from their deceitful and tempting flavour. But as forty years ago it was not unusual for matrons to get *muzzy*, nay *fou* on such occasions, the simple fact of Bessy's being only like her neighbours at those merry-makings cannot detract from the merits of her character.

Bessy was twenty-eight years of age when her master died. His widow soon followed her husband to the grave, and Bessy returned to reside with her mother, although it was with reluctance she was permitted, seeing she had now become a frequenter of *Tent Preachings*, which the old woman abhorred, and was more than ordinarily celebrated among the country-lads for the rosy beauty of her countenance, and the *mellifluence* of her breath. Shortly after she returned to dwell with her mother, a rich Moss-Laird paid his humble respects to Bessy, but her wooer, as she said, was so indifferent to THE Gospel, as expounded from the "Tents o' Logie, Leckro', Dunblane, an' ither godly places," that, in justice to her own religious habits and character, she could not do otherwise than reject his addresses. Scandalous detraction at the time would, that Bessy Stein never had it in her power to reject the suit of " Auld Gagram," but *certes* " Haly Bessy " was incapable of uttering a falsehood on this score, for many years afterwards she acknowledged *at a dredgy* that she could not refrain from weeping bitterly all that night she had pronounced the *nineteenth* NO, and her suitor taken, with tears, the final leave.

But Bessy Stein was *ordeened*, as she often observed, for matrimony, although other ten weary years elapsed after the affair with " Gagram," before " her ain " appeared. By this time Bessy's hopes of a husband had become very faint, and in her moments of peevish irritation she had been heard to mutter that even "the Bob o' Dunblane " were preferable to "the Life of Jenkin's Hen." "Hey— how," she would say to herself, " fool that I was to refuse Auld Gagram—a hale, stout, rauckle-carle—Hech—how— hum." By this time too, Bessy, in addition to her other accomplishments, had acquired the habit of taking snuff, and kept a supply in her bosom. The crimson flush that erewhile glowed in her countenance had threatened to betake itself into red streaky channels, and the rubicund hue of her nose had all but improved; yet, as she used to say, "what's ordeened will come to pass," for a timely remittance of two hundred pounds from an uncle in London enabled Bessy to renew her *cordial* enjoyments, and immediately afterwards a host of bachelors were suing for her hand. Bessy now determined " to make *her* hay while the sun shone," and accordingly selected, with her usual sagacity, a simple Moss-Farmer, originally from Kilbryde—a man of great honest worth, some means, and, in his younger years, a great admirer and frequenter of *Tent Preachings*. Some four years after her marriage, Bessy had the happiness of presenting her husband with two girls, who, nevertheless that no " son and heir " was ever afterwards forthcoming, added much to her felicity.

Bessy some years after this, from perhaps necessity, began to increase the quantity of her morning *cordial*, and in consequence the influence of the *spirit* became more apparent in her walk and conversation. One cold Sabbath forenoon, Bessy, before going to church, had rather *exceeded* than otherwise, and, as bad luck would have it, the minister that day, at the close of his sermon, read a lecture to his hearers, condemning, in no measured terms, *Promiscuous dancing* and *Smuggled whisky!*—the former as having a most immoral tendency among youth, and the latter as destructive of the interests of the fair-trader, prejudicial to the King's revenue, and *ruinous to the souls* of all such as encouraged the traffic, by purchasing the contraband *article*. Bessy having the very week before sent her two girls to a dancing-school in the vicinity of the manse; being invariably in the habit of preferring " Highlan' whisky " to " the muckle-stell trash;" and, above all, being at the time under the influence of an extra dose " dying within her," she imagined the whole denunciation to be levelled at herself. Just as the minister had closed, up she got, shook her clenched fist in his face, and, in a menacing tone roared out—" *Ye hypocrite, ye drink smuggled whisky yersel', and naething else if ye can get it; yer ain dochters are learned to dance—what ails you at me?"* It is needless to say that this interruption on Bessy's part amazed and petrified the audience. The minister, on recovering from his astonishment, meekly-wise, ordered the good woman to be conveyed home, for, to his certain knowledge, he said, *from excess of religious study and meditation,* she sometimes laboured under an aberration of mind. After this Bessy had numerous "conflicts with Satan." More frequently than ever did she attend "the Preachin's o' Logie, Lecropt, Dunblane, Stirling, and other places," where she had long been distinguished for her sanctimonious appearance at "the Tent," but, as she said, "the Evil Enemy" was always present with her, striving to neutralize the effect of "the Word upon her heart." On those occasions Bessy might be seen sitting on the green-sward, shutting her eyes to keep them from wandering, and shaking her head as the *mittimus* of the wicked, and the horrors of their future state, were denounced and depicted in words of thunder to the assemblage.

As Bessy advanced in years, and her daughters grew up, she became exceedingly anxious to increase her store, so as to be enabled to *buy* religious and *rich* husbands for her progeny. Satan, her inveterate enemy, continue our oralists, had the advantage in his struggles with her, while in the pursuit of this object. She is allowed to have used means rather unjust and prejudicial to her husband's relatives, in her endeavours to amass money for her daughters. But of this she afterwards sincerely repented. "Ah, Sirs! Ah, Sirs!" she would say to her daughters—"the love o' money is the root o' a' evil. I got a' uncle Robin's siller; an' his *house* too, that *anither* had a better right to—an' a' for *you,* ye trollops: I canna restore seven-fold accordin' to the word—may a' that's gude forgi'e me!" Indeed, but for the *cordial* in those moments of remorse, we are told, Bessy would have certainly expired. A generous glass, however, readily put matters to rights, having invariably the effect of dissolving Bessy's self-reproach into tears, thus affording comfortable and timely relief.

Bessy and her husband (we are now, from the scantiness of our materials, only able to add) removed from their farm to Dunblane, about the year 1791, accompanied by their daughters, one of whom was a widow without issue, and the other unfortunate enough to be unmarried. Here the two old people died some years afterwards—the father honoured as a man of strict integrity, honesty, and sobriety, and the mother, discovered at last, exactly the reverse. Their two daughters, after their death, "sold their possessions," got married *in one day* to *two brothers*, and immediately afterwards embarked for the States of America, since which period they have never been heard of.

II.

SANDY ROBIESON.

THIS harmless individual was born in Glendochart, near Killin, in 1753, and, after a life chequered with good and bad fortune, died at the age of seventy-seven, in rather indigent circumstances, at D——, on the 27th October, 1830.

Early initiated into all the superstitious mysteries then prevalent in his "native vale," in his boyhood repeatedly immersed in the celebrated *linn* of St. Fillan's, and naturally possessing a wayward disposition, it will not be deemed strange that he should, in many respects, appear to differ from ordinary mortals in the same humble walk of life. It is thus that his "weary pilgrimage" affords many traits of character to mark him out as a singular being.

The parents of this old man were "honest and *true*," and their son inherited their virtues. The deadly claymore of his father was plied with terrible effect in the ranks of "Prince Charlie" at Tranent, Falkirk, and Culloden; and consequently his son could not be expected, through the course of his life, to feel otherwise than a *bias* to that cause, for which his daring progenitor suffered so much. Saunders used to tell the writer of this, with much simplicity, that when about seven years of age, he was seized with a certain cutaneous malady, peculiar to the north in those days, which, from the improper use of charms, spells, *brimstonic unction*, and other *cures*, deprived him for a time of the use of his limbs. He was in consequence, he said, pronounced *elf-shot* by the old women who frequented his mother's house—and nothing short of nine immersions in St. Fillan's Linn was deemed necessary to restore him to health and the use of his legs. He was accordingly removed in a frame of wicker-work to the pool, and dipped nine times in succession over head and ears. Saunders recollected well this circumstance, and acknowledged that the "fricht" did him more good than the water, for in a short time afterwards he "was hale, lith and limb." Afterwards, he voluntarily, at stated intervals, performed *ablution* at St. Fillan's, so long as he remained in the neighbourhood. At the age of twelve, he became cow-herd to a farmer in Strathallan, and at sixteen he was *little-man* on a farm in the vicinity of Logie. At twenty, he was *muckle-man* on the same farm, and completely equipped in the garb of the Lowlands. In course of the next five years, he contrived to save some trifle of money, and in his twenty-fifth year he fell deeply in love. The object of his attachment was, what he called, "a bonny mountain rose" of the Ochils, but his addresses were rejected with all the coquetry and ridicule peculiar to her character. It was in vain poor Sandy told her of St. Fillan's water-kelpies and heather, and of the mighty prowess of his forbears in bloody battle. Distressed and disappointed, he determined to leave the Lowlands for ever, and shortly afterwards opened a small shop in Killin, where he became enamoured of one of his own fair country girls, and was not rejected; but, alas, the proud spirit of clanship creating some differences betwixt them, the match was broken off. Sandy once more "packed up his all," left Killin in disgust, and settled in the vicinity of Logie. Here, in a small apartment, he deposited his *bulziements* and money, working a *day's-darg* to any person that gave him employment. No Lothario had as yet captivated the heart of his quondam sweetheart, the "Ochil-rose," but Sandy was too proud to renew his old love-suit, or he would certainly have been now successful. Shortly after he returned to Logie, Sandy, at a Stirling May-fair, became enamoured of a bouncing, active, hearty quean, from D——, an heiress too, and one who frankly and at once declared that

"Tho' father and mither, an' a' should gae mad,"

he would find her ready and willing, on a day's notice, to

"Buckle up her hammell'd gear, and wi' him rin awa'."

Sandy and Jean had, in consequence, the very Sunday following, a jaunt to Glasgow, where they were married (the certificates of publication of the banns being forwarded after them by a friend), in the teeth of a strong opposition on the part of the bride's relatives, and much to the mortification and chagrin of a rich Strathallan farmer, who had deemed that the heiress of D—— would be won betwixt himself and his antagonist, another monied wooer. Immediately falling heir to considerable property by his wife, Sandy unluckily thought his head was now fairly above the mist, and that he had sufficient wherewithal to make him independent for life. But Sandy was too sanguine and inexperienced, and consequently unfortunate. A numerous family sprung up around him, and Sandy's property in the course of twenty years, was reduced to a small plot of clayey soil, and "without a house to put his head in." This was hard enough, but he had been only unfortunate, never dishonest, and he was not indebted to human being a single farthing. In this dilemma his mechanical genius did not forsake him. Rousing up his northern spirit, and collecting his scattered wits, he commenced brick-maker, and in a short time his bricks became celebrated over the country, from the tact which he had acquired in burning them thoroughly. But his "clay ran done," and his spirit became once more involved in gloom, not, however, until he had reared, with his own hands, a house to shield himself and family from the surliness of the storm. This "Castle" was built betimes of the bricks manufactured by himself, and considering the self-taught architect and builder, and the fact of there being neither plummet nor line used in the rearing of it, the appearance, although uncouth, is far from contemptible. This *biggin'* is two storeys high, is divided into no less than eight different apartments, and considering the many bombardments which its citadel has experienced during the dotage of its founder, its walls may be said to have lost little of their original *perpendicular*, and its chimney-tops nothing of their most perfect *equilibrium*.

After this Saunders became a day labourer, and maintained his family as well as he could. During all their vicissitudes of fortune, it was remarked that his wife never uttered a complaint, never reproaching her husband with the failure of his projects, which, to better his circumstances, were many, and generally ended in disappointment and loss. Jean was, indeed, a "help meet" for Sandy, always cheerful, always willing to fight with the world to assist her husband through his difficulties. She still survives, "hale and hearty," in the house built by her husband; and old as she is, her noble and independent spirit remains unbroken and unsubdued, notwithstanding the many "ups and downs" she has experienced in life.

III.

HENRY REID.

WITHIN the dark, windowless walls of his solitary cottage, situated among the duskiness of surrounding plantations of fir-wood, by the drove-road side, about a mile above Greenloaning, where he had resided, secluded and alone, for the space of twenty-eight years, died Henry Reid, in the eighty-ninth year of his age. No human being saw him breathe his last. He was found on the forenoon of Saturday, the 7th November, 1829, with his clothes partly on, reclining on a block of wood, sleeping the sleep of death, by one of his nearest neighbours. He could not, however, have been long dead, as his body, when discovered, was still warm at the breast, and the extremities only chilly cold. He had apparently fallen from his chair, and, it is supposed, a stroke of paralysis or apoplexy may have terminated his existence without a struggle.

This old man was so remarkable for his eccentricities and singular habits that the writer of this is sure that a small space, occupied with a hasty sketch of his more prominent features, cannot fail to prove acceptable to many, and to none more so than those who were acquainted with the individual himself, and the peaceable inoffensive life which he led. It may be mentioned that the peculiarities which stamped Henry Reid at first sight as a "character" seem to have been hereditary, for it is questionable whether his father, a brother, and two sisters, were not still more remarkable than himself. His parents dying about 1760, left him, his brother, and two sisters, all decidedly misanthropic, in possession of the small pendicle which Henry retained till his death. So long as the sisters lived, they literally screamed when a stranger of the male sex ventured to cross their threshold. Soon, however, after the death of their parents they dropped one by one into the grave, and John and Henry were left to manage matters, both "out an' in," as they best could. Henry acted the part of dairy-maid. It was he who managed the cow, fed her, milked her, and made the butter and cheese, kept the fences in repair, and attended to everything connected with the pendicle. John, on the other hand, being an excellent *theeker*, earned as much through the year as paid the rent of their few acres. In 1801 John took ill and died, and Henry was left without a friend on earth. He still, however, found means to keep the pendicle, and contrived to earn as much by cutting wood, and making pailing-stobs, in the neighbouring woods, as paid his rent; and he did so regularly for twenty-four years after his brother's death. Four years ago his poor circumstances and great age being represented to his landlord, that gentleman was generously pleased to intimate to him that no rent would in future be exacted from him. This timely assistance revived the drooping frame and sinking spirits of the old man, and he could not restrain the tears of gratitude. It was remarked when he died his *all* was worn out and done. He had sold his cow some months before his death, and deposited her price with a friendly neighbour in order to defray, as he said, the expense of his funeral, which indeed it did. His fire-wood was almost exhausted; his razor lay on the *back-stane*, blunt, tinged with rust, and useless; his spectacles were observed on the same place, the case worn out, and wanting one of the glasses, and the other shattered and broken. His bedstead was frail rotten lumber, and his bedding perfectly threadbare and in tatters. Scarcely a particle of food kind was within his door but what was found in his pockets, being a small portion of bread and cheese. Indeed, for some months before his death, he was necessarily more frequently to be seen at the houses of neighbouring benefactors, where his "tales of other years" made him always a welcome guest, and whence he never returned home with an empty stomach.

Henry, although never fortunate enough to get married, was far from being insensible to the charms of female beauty; yet he was timid and bashful in the extreme. Groups of country lasses frequently assembled at his humble abode, in the harvest evenings, for amusement, when Henry, even at the frosty age of seventy, was seen to fall in love with one or other of his visitors. Wrapped in his wide *rachan*, with his best broad bonnet on his head, and his new *gramashes* drawn over his knees, he might be seen, after night-fall, sauntering about the doors of some farm-steading, where one of his fair favorites resided, taking a peep through the window, and skulking in corners, as if afraid of being discovered.

In order to form some idea of Henry's peculiarities and predilections for the utmost simplicity in everything, we have only to look a century back, and record something of the father as related by the son. Henry venerated the memory of his parent, and imitated him in most of his original characteristics. The whole body of Henry's progenitor being in all weathers enveloped in a loose suit of the coarsest home-made cloth, his outer man presented the most uncouth and shaggy appearance. The set of buttons on his coat were two inches in diameter. The shoes he wore were made by himself, which he finished with a studding of tackets, and heels and toe-caps of iron, and, to *crown* the whole, a monstrously large broad bonnet surmounted his shaggy head. When this man got married, and obtained a lease of his pendicle, there was then no cottage attached to it. This was only the work of a few days to the simple architect. In the course of a single week a *biggin'*, of as a primitive a description as can well be conceived, was ready for the reception of its constructor, his wife, and his cow. Henry used to give the following description of it to the writer of this:—The side walls were six feet high, four feet at the base, and two at the top. They consisted of alternate layers of *feal*, and flat stones as *bands;* the gavels were six feet thick at least, and rose in the common way. The rude undressed trees of the roof, termed *couples*, were fixed in the earth at the bottom of the walls, and secured *side-wa' height*, with cross beams or *bauks*, which were fastened to the couple-legs with large wooden pins driven through one and a-half inch *wimble-bores*. Next across the couple-legs were laid two *rungs* on each side of the roof, and a *rigging-tree* on the top. Then there were laid on the *kebars*, parallel to the couple-legs, next a slating of *divots*, and last of all a coating of *bog-thack*, and a ridging of flax-mill dust. An aperture of no small dimensions was left in the middle of the ridge to admit the light and "vent the reek." No "winnock-bunker" was otherwise considered necessary. A circular tube of wicker-work, plastered with clay, surmounted the "hole i' the riggin'," which was with no impropriety called the *lum-head*. The door was a frame of basket-work also, and finished with clay.

In this humble hovel, betwixt the years 1730 and 1741, the whole family were born, and instructed by their father to read the Bible. Here the two daughters died, and here the two brothers lived after their sisters' death, until the old *crazy bield*, one stormy night was blown about their ears, they and the cow narrowly escaping destruction. They were then furnished by the proprietor of their pendicle with a more comfortable habitation; yet such was their antipathy to windows that they immediately built them up as soon as they took possession. Here John died, and here Henry also, "the last of his race." To close this sketch of these originals, let it be told they were all honest and industrious; and we cannot forbear regretting that

Henry did not survive a few years longer, that we might have had an opportunity of availing ourselves of a few more of his ancient oral tales.

IV.

THE MUCKLE WIFE O' BITHERGIRSE.

THE following graphic sketch of Bithergirse, from the pen of the celebrated Josephus Chalmers, Esq., may previously be not unacceptable to the readers of The Muckle Wife o' Bithergirse:—

"The little huddled hamlet of Bittergirse, Buttergrass, or Bithergirse, stands, or as a native of Bithergirse would say, *curs* on the brow of a muir about a Scots mile, or thereby, south of Blackford, Perthshire. According to tradition, the Muir of Bithergirse was ceded to the patriarch of a band of gypsies, by the *Gudeman o' Ballengeich*, who, in one of his *incog.* excursions through his kingdom, fell in with the group about the spot where Bithergirse was subsequently built; and, becoming enamoured of 'the Tinkers' occupation,' thought it only just and right that an especial mark of his royal regard should be conferred on the *Caird* and his progeny. The King accordingly granted to him and his daughter a charter of right to the Muir of Bithergirse, to subsist 'while wood grew and water ran,' and also to their heirs for ever, upon presenting to the Scottish king, when he passed that way, *a ram-horn spoon* and a *dish of Kaily-brose*. Be this as it may, true it is, that the inhabitants of Bithergirse appear to be, at this day, a distinct race of beings from their neighbours—'The Tykes o' Ogilby' not excepted. Their dialect differs considerably from that of all around them; and scholars have been heard to aver, that traces of the ancient Coptic may yet be discovered in several of their phrases. They wear clothes differently fashioned from those of any other tribe in the known world. The men have a sort of body-coat not longer than a ploughman's jacket, admirably fitted to cast the rain-drop over their posteriors, with a couple of large buttons close to each other behind, and placed betwixt the arm-pits. Such of them as wear hats have the brims scooped up all around, with a semi-globular crown, resembling a bee-skep. The *breech* of these mortals, from the circumstance of their upper garments being so curtailed—without any stretch of imagination, particularly when the hinder parts of their buttock-clothing become thread-bare,—may be likened to the face of a huge owl, as they waddle along at a little distance from an observer. The women wear a short-gown, which they call a *Tosh*, which is generally of coarse home-made plaiding, *litted* blue by themselves, and fashioned so as to tie behind. Their petticoats, of the same stuff, like the men's *coatties*, are sorely scanty in longitude,—and lest their limbs should catch cold, they are securely encircled with ample *huggars*. The young women allow their hair to flaunt about their ears, and the heads of the matrons are enveloped in large pieces of cloth of a tawny colour, which they term *Hoos*. The folks of Bithergirse keep themselves by themselves as much as possible, and look upon strangers with Creolian suspicion. In August last, 'mine host' at Blackford, having learned something of my object in visiting Perthshire, requested me to accompany him to Bithergirse, as a place in a truly primitive state. He told me there was no road either to or from Bithergirse, but he knew 'whereabouts it lay.' 'What,' said I, 'no road either to or from it—do the people never go to church or market?' 'No, no,' he replied,' 'they have *Reverends* and *Right Reverends* of their own—both Teachers and Preachers—they live on their own produce—and for *roads*, it has long been a common saying here, that there's *nae* road either *tae* or *frae* Bithergise.' Early on the following morning my landlord and I found ourselves on what he called 'Tarny-Hill,' in full view of Bithergirse. Having taken a sketch of the place, which really was as difficult to do justice to as the Great Cave of Staffa, we descended the hill to see *the folks* of Bithergirse. On a nearer view, the hovels appeared, many of them to be very ancient, and to have been rebuilt and repaired repeatedly on the old sites, with due regard to what must have been the *original plan*, as laid down by the Patriarch of Bithergirse, upon receiving his charter, and laying off his *city*. No such thing could I discern about Bithergirse as a *right*-angle, a *straight*-line, a *perpendicular*, or a *level*. Not two houses, or two things alike—all irregularity. The hamlet, indeed, appeared to have been tossed from the clouds, concentrated by a hurricane, or *sown* by a whirlwind. Fronting every point of the compass, and accommodating themselves to the irregularities of the ground, the groups of huts may be likened to a horde of non-descript and clumsy animals, couchant on a brae—with *riggins* like dromedaries' backs —mottled walls like the sides of panthers, and *lum-heads*, rolled round with straw-ropes, resembling the heads of so many polar-bears. The smoke that morning issued in dense columns from every door and window-hole, and I was told that the principal fuel used was turf and *dried cow-dung*, collected during summer by the children in the fields. I learned, too, that twenty years ago there was not a lock on a door, nor a pane of glass in all Bithergirse."

Thus far, Mr. Chambers, who wrote in 1810. Now for our memoir of the Muckle Wife of Bithergirse, in 1835 :—

Mary Carr, as she called herself, became a residenter in Bithergirse about 1790. She had been coming and going about Bithergirse frequently before that time, in the character of a retailer of small wares; but in 1792 she had taken a little hut, and was retailing *swine-seam, brimstone*, and *louse-traps* to the folks of Bithergirse. Nobody knew the place of her nativity and of her lineage; all in

F

Bithergirse were equally in the dark, for she studiously maintained a profound silence regarding the place of her birth and all her relations. Mary might be nearly forty years of age at the time she became resident in the place. In stature she was a perfect Colossus—muscular, well made, active, lusty, and strong; and in all the surrounding district, which she frequently travelled, hawking "flour-bread" and "gathering eggs," she was universally styled "The Muckle Wife o' Bithergirse." Such of the *Reverends* of Bithergirse as were conversant in Bible history thought Mary to be a descendant of a daughter of Anak, while "Auld Davy Eadie" and "Punler the tailor," who had picked up some profound information from a stray volume of voyages, which they had borrowed from " Niel M'Leod, the Papist," believed Mary to have been an import from Patagonia, and brought to Scotland by the "*Great Navygaator, Strait Mac-gallon.*" But wherever Mary was born, she took very good care to say nothing about it. In course of her truck with the wives of Bithergirse, Mary contrived not only to earn a comfortable livelihood, but " to lay by something for a sair foot," before many years of her residence elapsed. She sold, in addition to the *staple-commodities* above-mentioned, tobacco-pipes, stocking-wires, powder and shot, and flints for " the gunners," and secretly, for the accommodation of the wives of Bithergirse, *a wee drap real Highlan' thing*, and tea. In exchange for the latter, the Muckle Wife o' Bithergirse was frequently under the necessity of taking *dunts o' cheese* and *clatches o' butter*, for the men of Bithergirse early *felt* that it would be absolutely requisite to hold the purse-strings themselves in the neighbourhood " o' sic an awfu' muckle wife" as " The Muckle Wife o' Bithergirse." But it had, perhaps, been better for their own interests had the men of Bithergirse left their wives the continued unrestricted care of the *siller*, for the Muckle Wife throve in proportion as the money became scarcer among the pendiclers' and farmers' wives of the Muir of Bithergirse. Mary's traffic, after the *embargo* was laid upon the *siller*, was necessarily transacted in the *dark*. One farmer's wife, more than ordinarily ingenious in a *thirsty* emergency, used to pack the water-stoups with butter and cheese, over which she would *tramp* a thick layer of oatmeal, leaving as much room on the top of each as to contain a choppin or so of *sour-milk*. She would then find ways and means to have the "twa stoups o' sour milk" sent to the Muckle Wife o' Bithergirse—"puir body, as she had na a cow to gie her sowp." All these things Mary turned, by some means or other, to good account. She went through the country generally two days in each week, besides going often to Stirling on Fridays, to dispose of her eggs and truck with her Cowane Street cronies. She seldom travelled without a *wee drap* slung about her person, which was often contained in a "*half-moon* flask," almost encircling her huge body. She is believed by the folks of Bithergirse to have been among the first, if not the very first, to discover the great convenience of using bladders in vending *mountain-dew* by itinerant spirit-dealers. Mary was, indeed, a woman of much sagacity—always sly and cautious. She was kind too, for a *dry* customer never was at a loss to banish the blue-devils in Mary's spence. And if she knew the applicant to be *honourable*, she would not only treat him to a bumper from her *ain bottle*, but would *tick* to the extent of a tappit-hen before her drouthy friend were permitted to depart *unslockened*. These *scores* she recorded in hieroglyphics on the bed-end with chalk—half a *circle* denoting sixpence, an O a shilling, a double O two, &c. The Muckle Wife o' Bithergirse, it was allowed, was frequently in danger of being *deceived* into marriage by some of those *tick* customers; but as Mary never drank spirits herself the report is probably without foundation.

Our Muckle Wife had dealt about ten years without opposition in Bithergirse before any other in her line had started. At last, however, in the person of "Tam the Horner," she had to contend not only with a resolute, clever, dare-devil, sort of fellow, but with what in those days was rare in Bithergirse, and unknown among spoon-makers—the Muckle Wife o' Bithergirse had to contend with a *scholar*. Tam had been descended of respectable parents in Edinburgh, and being an only child received a liberal education. He was intended for the church, but nothing else would Tam be but a tinsmith. Having served his apprenticeship, about the expiry of which his parents dying, and leaving a little money, he commenced business for himself, and in the course of a year became bankrupt. Leaving Edinburgh with an old horse and cart, his tools and the wreck of his fortune, he commenced itinerant, or as some of the gypsy-girls, who followed in his train, expressed it, "a travelling tinsmith;" and but for that "waefu' whisky" had soon permanently bettered his circumstances. In 1802, Tom's *encampment* appeared in the vicinity of Bithergirse, comprising several tents, carts and cuddy-asses, with a motley variety of men, women, and children. The Muckle Wife o' Bithergirse remarked, on witnessing the extent of Tam's establishment, that in all her travels through braid Scotland she had never seen at one place so many *cuddies* except on the Castlehill of Stirling. An intercourse very shortly subsisted betwixt Tam and the Muckle Wife o' Bithergirse. Tam had money always, and the Muckle Wife "aye the wee drap real thing." A thought, however, suddenly struck Tam, and he resolved to *pit in the pin* for a twelvemonth. Making money with all his art and all his might, he soon found himself in circumstances to clothe himself respectably, and to take a lease of one of the domiciles of Bithergirse, after having maintained headquarters on the Muir for six months. Very soon Tam's hut presented a perfect galaxy of tin goods—pans, basins, pitchers, watering-pans, and smugglers' flasks dangled all around, exhibiting a sheen of beauty hitherto unknown in Bithergirse. The Muckle Wife soon became alarmed. Tam's train scoured the country with their cuddy-creels, exchanging their pans, &c., for meal, butter, cheese, and money where it could be had, and collecting the whole poultry and eggs in the district. Besides, he determined to give a death-blow to Mary's principal source of profit, for no other reason, he said, than in revenge for the bitter enmity and ill-will which she evidently bore towards him. Bartering with the smugglers—giving them flasks in exchange for whisky,— he began to oppose Muckle Mary on her own favourite ground, with success. He sold the whisky in Bithergirse for money or goods, vended it by means of a favourite, who drove an ass through the country; and, but for his untimely death, had certainly superseded the *use* of the Muckle Wife o' Bithergirse longer about the place. But Tam died, poor fellow, and the Muckle Wife soon afterwards became *resuscitated* in all the plenitude of her bustle and glory. Another word about Tam. He had religiously abstained from drinking during the twelve months he had himself determined to *keep in the pin*, notwithstanding that he was amongst whisky "in opposing the Muckle Wife," several months before that term expired. Elated by a consciousness of having been able to resist the infatuation of drinking, and this for a whole year, he unfortunately thought he might take a glass now with impunity. He did so, got drunk, and next morning was a corpse.

We are now arrived at the climacteric of the life of our massy heroine—the Muckle Wife o' Bithergirse. After poor Tam Horner's death Mary's business revived, and she became not only wealthy but very corpulent. Although now turned of fifty, it was not before this period that she had a goodly number of suitors, all anxious and willing really to make a *wife* of the Muckle Wife o' Bithergirse. About this time, when her *Chop* was frequently beleagured after night-fall with groups of wooers, the Muckle Wife o' Bithergirse began to feel some uneasiness about the probable result of an opposition in her secret-trade, which had just got a sort of footing on the *remains* of Tam the Horner, under the auspices of Lucy Arnot, a native of Bithergirse. But Lucy she got early rid of in an unexpected and agreeable manner. An old widower, from the neighbourhood of Greenloaning, had several times *dandered* all the way to Bithergirse for *stocking-wires*, in moonlight evenings. He had, it appears, taken it into his head that it would save him some trouble, besides loss of time, if he could prevail on the Muckle Wife to accompany him with her stock of wires to the heather, and hinted this accordingly; but the Muckle Wife o' Bithergirse excused herself, on the ground that he was too young for her, recommending him, however, to explain himself to Lucy Arnot, who, she said, had a "guid stock o' *stockin'-wires*," besides being on the carpet—young, plump, and ready for wedlock. Under such circumstances, placed as Lucy was, in direct opposition in *the secret line* to the Muckle Wife o' Bithergirse, and not unlikely to be successful in trade, nothing could certainly be more gratifying to the Muckle Wife than to learn the fact that the old muirland carle had taken her advice—applying to Lucy for *stocking-wires* that very night before going home, and finally of having taken possession of the *citadel* by storm— removing his bride and her *stocking-wires* to the land of heather—thus demolishing the ramparts of a dangerous and new opposition to the very profitable traffic carried on by the Muckle Wife o' Bithergirse. Our Muckle Wife never got married, although between her fiftieth and sixtieth year she had it frequently in her power to form a matrimonial alliance, and with good matches too. The old stocking-worker who carried Lucy Arnot captive by dint of money, would willingly have married her, and he was a man worth some thousand pounds, but shrivelled, old, and miserable.

The last offer Mary had was the hand of "Auld Johnny Fenton," a rich old body of Bithergirse. The Muckle Wife o' Bithergirse was just sixty years of age when one day, as she sat at her wheel, in pops the little bonnet of auld Johnny Fenton, an individual some ten years older than herself. "Presaarve us, Johnny!" exclaimed the Muckle Wife o' Bithergirse, "What win's blawn you this airt the day—war ye e'er in my *Chop* afore, Johnny Fenton?" and she laid her hand on the rim of her wheel to hear him speak, and listening in dead silence, stared Johnny through her *nose-specks* full in the face. "Deed, Mary," said Cocky Fenton, as he leaned him down on the *creepy* by the fire, "I hae na been i' yer house this towmond, but I dreamt sic a queer dream about you yestreen that I had nae peace till I cam yont to tell ye't." "Yer no thinkin' am a witch or a spaewife, or a reader o' cups, or giftit intil sic things as the *tarpitin* a dreams, are ye, that ye come to tell me yer dreams, Johnny?" said the Muckle Wife o' Bithergirse, reclining forward over her *heck*, and eyeing him sternly. "O, no, no, Mary," said Cocky Fenton, "nae sic things atweel, but I'm thinkin' ye'll can tell me if my dream sud ever come to pass;" and after a short pause he looked up from the stool at Mary, and added, with a grin peculiar to himself, and in a measured undertone, "I dreamt *you an' me were married*, woman." "And *beddit*, Johnny?" said the Muckle Wife o' Bithergirse, mimicking his voice. "No, no, Mary," replied Johnny Fenton, "it had na come that length e'er I waken'd." "An' *never shall*, Johnny," said the Muckle Wife o' Bithergirse. "What! my *wee*, silly, auld mannie, what wad *ye* do wi' sic a wife 's *me?*—there's no as muckle creish about ye a' as wad weigh a fardin' can'le—ye wad be a poor bed-fellow to me, indeed. I wad smore ye man, an' ne'er ken I did it, or tyne ye amang the blankets—gae wa', gae wa'—as the sang says,—

'An auld stumpie bodie sall never get me.'"

And round went the wheel-rim faster than ever, as she lilted a stanza. Johnny did not yet lose courage, however. He was old enough to remember the proverb—" Bitin' an' scartin' is Scots folks wooin'." So after a fidge or two, and giving his palms another *birsle* at the Muckle Wife's ingle, he resumed his place in his *tete-a-tete* with the Muckle Wife o' Bithergirse. "Just stop yer wheel a minute mair, Mary," said Johnny; and Mary again laid her hand on the rim. "I'm surely no sae *wee's* a' that, Mary," quoth Johnny, laughing. "I dinna think ye wad either *smore me or tyne me amang the claes*. Mary, ye ken I've plenty o' siller;"—"And *I* dinna want, Johnny," said Mary, interrupting him. "But," said Johnny, anxiously, "ye ken we pay *twa* rents—*ae* house might haud us baith—*ae* fire an' *ae* pat sair us baith—and ye ken *your* hugger and *my* hugger coupit intil ane wad be sure to keep us confartable as lang's we leeve." "But, Johnny Fenton," said the Muckle wife o' Bithergirse, gruffly, "I'll just tell ye for guid an' a', that if ever I tak a man, it sall be a richt ane—a muckle heavy chiel like mysel,—nane o' yer auld maukin-hippit withered bodies for me. Sae tak that to *yersel'*, Johnny Fenton, an' come nae mair to me wi' yer daft auld lees, an' yer dreamin' nonsense." This tirade was a perfect killer to auld Cocky Fenton. He said not a word more, and after seizing his nose with his shrivelled thumb and fingers, and snorting in his palm, he rose slowly from his seat and silently retired. "What think ye o' auld Cocky Fenton," said the Muckle Wife o' Bithergirse to a neighbour woman, who just came in as Johnny went out. "The daft auld doitred little ghaist cam ance errand, he said, to tell me that he dreamt yestreen *him an' me were married;*" and she put her "waly nieves" in her haunches, heaved like a convulsed mountain, and belched like an elephant.

But our *materiel* is nearly exhausted, and our memoir of the Muckle Wife o' Bithergirse must necessarily draw to a close. The Muckle Wife enjoyed good health for several years after this, but when she did fail, "she came down like snaw aff a dyke." She is related to have been "sweer, sweer, to dee," by our authorities. "Bring down the beuks," said the *Reverend* one night he visited the Muckle Wife o' Bithergirse on her death-bed. "Hooly, hooly, awee," said the Muckle Wife o' Bithergirse, faintly from the bed—"*lat the beuks abee*, an' crack a while langer about *wild-beass an' things*—it's ill eneuch, but it's no come to *that* o't yet." But after this, when she *felt* that shortly die she must, she executed a deed of settlement, bequeathing some two hundred pounds to a few of her more indigent acquaintances. And maintaining a profound silence with regard to her birth and parentage till the last, the Muckle Wife o' Bithergirse departed this life a few days afterwards. She died in 1815, and was decently interred in the church-yard of Blackford, where a handsome monumental stone, erected by her legatees, now marks her grave.

V.

AULD WILLIE O' THE BACK-HILLS.

WILLIE STEVENSON, the subject of the present memoir, is no fictitious character. His faults were not of that bad and by-all-abhorred kind, that to pourtray them to the world we are under the necessity of laying the scene at Bithergirse, and sketching Willie under another name. Willie Stevenson long possessed the sheep-farm of Backhills, in the Ochils, as honest and hearty an old fellow as ever told a story or drank a gill. His only known fault was that he sometimes took what he called "awfu' *spates* o' drink," when he had occasion to go south to Tillicoultry, or north to Blackford. He had two sons—Jamie and Sandy—true "Chips of the Old Block." Jamie was the principal shepherd, and Sandy had the charge under him, not merely because he was the younger brother, but because the old man had, he said, more confidence in Jamie's carefulness—"although he took a gude rough glass"—than that of his brother. Sandy took *great spates* like his father—becoming *dry* in all weathers, at periodical times. "Ye lippen owre muckle to Providence, Sandy," the old man would say when Sandy returned, having left his charge for a week to drink a score of hogs at *Girzy Heatheriquick's* of the Cross-keys—"what if it had come on a storm o' drift, and smored a' the sheep, man, and you awa'? Ye should hae ta'en them a' wi' ye man—better ye had drucken them a' man, than rin the risk o' losing them a' thegither amang the snaw—they wad a done somebody gude." "'Deed, faither," Sandy would say, " if a thing *be* gaun to be lost, lost it *will be*, although ye had it in yer plaid; the sheep's a' safe an' so am *I*, the twa three crook-yowes war for nae use bit sell—an'—but say nae mair about it—noo when it's by." The old man, aware of his own weakness, and erroneously believing such drunken predilections to be *in the blood*, and hereditary, would say, indeed, "nae mair," only he would caution Sandy, "for ony sake, to do as weel's he could," for "him that did *a'* he could," he would add, "would *whiles do mair*." Jamie, too, took what he called "a *Gell*," but *two days* slockened him, and, as he expressed it, "kept him from *geyzenin*" for several months. Auld Willie, like many other *thirsty* mortals, was frequently at a loss for *siller*, although he never wanted means. When he became dry, he would just step over the hill to Tillicoultry, west to *Auld Shirra-Muir's* or *Maggy o' the Bog's*, and commence drinking, where he would sometimes continue for a week. The whisky-mongers of these places knew Willie's way, and that he would pay them *plack and fardin'*—"again' clippin' time," if they wanted wool, or with a few *crook-yowes*, when they chose to send for them. Nevertheless, of this foible, Auld Willie Stevenson bore a good character—he tippled none. When he drank he *did* drink, and when sober he was *really* so, drinking nothing stronger than the limpid spring, which abounded in all its cool purity among the hills. He was a clever man too, a good sheep farmer, and knew the markets well—how to buy, and how and when to sell. It was remarked that when Willie had any business ado at a distance from home, he drank no ardent spirits whatever—never any, moreover, when he had money upon him. He thought nothing of giving wool and crook-yowes for liquor, which he had *scored* in public-houses; but to part with money in such cases he would not, if possible. He never kept spirits in his house, well aware that although he had a bottle a "mile-deep" it would soon be drained. "The far'er frae the *deevil* the better," he would say, "Tillicoultry is *near* enough, lads—Blackford is near enough—an' that auld reekit jade, Maggy o' the Bog is *owre near*. Shirra-Muir's an honest auld cock, but he would drink Lochleven dry—nae man can stand him. *He* wad drink a hale *score* o' wathers in a week himsel." Willie's wife remarked that he never spoke of drinking—never mentioned the name of whisky in his family, except when on the eve of commencing the spate; that they knew as well as could be, from his manner and conversation a few days before he *took the hills*, but durst not speak, as in that case he became enraged.

Such is a sketch of this eccentric character, and such as it is, it is a true one. We shall only add that Willie died nearly twenty years ago, and that there are yet too many in that country-side, as well as many nearer to us, who are following, apparently irrecoverably too, in his wake.

VI.

MAGGY O' THE BOG.

"MAGGY'S" was a well-known *howf*, and for many years was much frequented by visitants to the Sheriffmuir, from Stirling, Dunblane, Blackford, and many other places. Her "gill an' bottle o' yill" were long famed for their quality, and her "leaf-bread, eggs, and butter," were frequently applied for by the way-worn traveller, in his solitary transit betwixt Blackford and Stirling, through the long bleak and weary muir. In her younger years, about 1745, Maggy is said to have been a "clever huzzy, an' a furthy quean;" and till the last, when she died in 1804, at the great age of ninety-nine, she retained her faculties. In all the drunken frolics and boisterous blustering battles which took place about *The Bog*, Maggy retained the most perfect composure, fearing, as she said, "neither man nor woman born, *if they keepit out o' her een.*" She gave birth to several stout fellows, by her husband, whose name was Wilson, and one daughter at least, Tibby, who succeeded her at death—all of whom now repose with their mother in the dust. The little house and yard which Maggy occupied had been possessed by her ancestors for many generations, and this without any rent being demanded or paid. Indeed, had Maggy's heirs thought proper to retain possession, they might have done so, and this with a *title* as valid as that conferred by any charter in Scotland—*undisturbed possession from time immemorial*. Maggy's house was situated some six unmeasured miles north-east of Stirling, on the muir-road to Blackford. It was a primitive hovel indeed. The gable faced the road, on which a few truals of lime had been scattered, to make the clumsy *effigies* of a bottle and glass more conspicuous, which Maggy had *painted* with her own fingers. Within, the hut was as miserable-looking and smoky as can be imagined. The *ceiling* was the *kebars*,

glistening with soot, which in soft weather dropped down
copiously on all below. There were a sort of two apartments, and two *lum-heads*, but their being a free intercourse
betwixt these above the *bed-heads*, the smoke issued from
both ends of the house at the same time, although one fire
only was kindled, the excess escaping by the door and
glassless window-chinks; yet in this uncouth *wigwam*
more whisky was sold during last century than can
perhaps possibly be conceived. Fishers, porters, carters
returning south with their empty carts, nay, gentlemen
from different distances around, met in Maggy's to *hold
the splore*. The remote situation, indeed, together with
the loneliness and pastoral quietness of the place—the
rudeness of the house itself—the antiquity and homeliness
of the furniture, and the kind simplicity of Maggy herself,
added to the reputed genuineness of the Highland whisky,
may have conspired to render her dwelling the favourite
resort of many in all ranks of society. It may be added,
that during the greater part of the last half of the
eighteenth century there was not a single British regiment
of the line cantoned in or about Stirling but knew Maggy
o' the Bog's, every man of them. On Sabbath-days, in
particular, in good weather, dozens of soldiers might be
seen at a time about Maggy's premises. Nevertheless, of
all the whisky she sold, Maggy never got rich. She indeed
brought up her family, fed them, and clothed them, while
they remained with her, which was no longer than they
were able to mount an old horse and bestride a pair of
casks—Maggy's sons having preferred being smugglers of
contraband tea and brandy from the West Highlands,
where it was landed by foreigners engaged in the traffic,
to everything else.

Maggy's son, John, afterwards known through most of
Scotland by the appellation of *Auld Shirra-moor*, was a
most noted dealer in this way. Many beatings did the
excisemen receive at his hands, and often and severely did

he suffer in his turn by fine and imprisonment. He was a robust, active, fearless man, and was long in good circumstances, but like almost all who dealt in intoxicating liquors, he became much reduced before death. Maggy's daughter, Tibby, after the old woman died, succeeded her in the Bog, retailing whisky, &c.; but her brother, *Auld Shirra-moor*, having obtained a small farm, a mile or so north from the place of his nativity, on which a house and offices were built, obtained a license to sell "British Spirits, Porter, and Ale," and Tibby's *change* failed considerably. The Bog had never been a licensed house, and the excise laws being now more rigorously enforced, Tibby was fined by the Justices until she had not a shilling. Her brother died in 1811, but another *vintner* succeeded him, who, paying a dear license himself, determined to oust Tibby if possible, or compel her to pay for a license as well as himself; but Tibby *saw him awa'*, and smuggled away a gill as usual, until 1828, when old age and infirmity compelled her to abandon both the Bog and whisky together, just in time to escape death, from the old house tumbling about her ears. Tibby died some years afterwards in Stirling, and *Maggy o' the Bog's* is now level with the neighbouring moor—not a stone of it above another.

VII.

THE BLACK LAIRD.

THIS man was by trade a tailor, and flourished when broad bonnets, large buttons, and hodden-gray were in fashion in Dunblane, and lived long after all those good articles of clothing had become *obsolete*. He saved money too, and left property, notwithstanding that the motto, "*A remnant shall be saved,*" was never by him, either virtually or *de facto*, acknowledged. He was mostly employed in the country, where he long wrought for fivepence a-day and "his meat." The laird used to start early and cheerfully on Monday morning from his own house, with his flute in his pocket and his goose and lapboard over his shoulder, and this for an employer's house many miles distant, where he would arrive before the family got up, and rouse the inmates at the window with one of his most lively airs. He never returned generally until Saturday evenings, having always at least a week's work before him near the same place. Indeed, in the Laird's time, tailors performed most of their work in the neighbourhood of towns and villages, itinerating through the country, and receiving, with their apprentices, board and lodgings in the houses of their employers. And when they did get work to do in their own houses, the Laird used to remark, with virtuous indignation, "they neither keepit a parin' nor a clippin' o' other folks claith, but sent a' hame wi' the claes, every patch an' thread owre stappit i' the pouches."

The Laird liked ill the new fashions—"*ae* way an' *a'* way." The new coats, he said, were "*nippit-things*, strait, swallow-tailed, bare, useless, mocks, and sae dear was that English thin trash, that nane but gentlemen sud buy it." He hated, too, the *perquisite* system, which became fashionable, he said, as honesty *dee'd awa'*, and people gave their clothes to make to a set of *new-fangled* scoundrels and *land-loupers frae gude-kens-whare*. It must be allowed, indeed, that in the Laird's day the craft to which he belonged were in general more reputable as men than at the present time. This may have been the case from their strict punctuality in returning every remnant of cloth over to their employers. In those days there were few phrases peculiar to the craft, and one could not have distinguished one Knight of the Bodkin amongst a thousand. The old tailors wore clean shirts, whole clothes, and were reputed for general cleanliness and integrity. Common bruit, now-a-days, will have it otherwise. The vulgar report says, that there is not such a mortal as a tailor free of vermin, unaddicted to *cabbage*, or one whose word can for a moment be believed. This cannot possibly be true, but still it will be allowed that "there is aye sim water whaur the stirk's drowned." Nay, indeed, in deference to the truth, it must be recorded that many tailors at the present time are known to have amassed much wealth by what is called *Cabbage*. The Laird, long before his death, foretold this, and never could understand by what infatuation *thae new tailzeurs* were admitted to offices of trust, as he believed it would be as easy for a tailor of the New-School to *put his goose through the eye of his needle* as to maintain a character for strict integrity, initiated as he necessarily would be, from the first, into all the mysteries of *Perquisitism*. Something must be allowed for the Laird here. Honest himself to the very core, and no doubt nettled a little that the good old fashions were discarded, and himself not so well employed as in his younger years, his opinion might be rashly formed, and as unguardedly expressed; yet he never could bear to see "ane o' thae lousy thieves at the Broad i' the Sabbath-day." He said "it might be a new plan to reform them that the De'il had pitten i' the minister's head;" but he would just ask, " Can the Ethiopian change his *skin*, or the leopard his *spots?*" Thus we have seen the Laird on one side of the leaf; let us now look at the other.

The Laird, like most of the citizens of Dunblane in those days, was very superstitious. His code of belief embraced the whole tribes of *ghaists, wraiths, water-kelpies,* and all the varieties of *bogles* and *fairies*. And he had, moreover, not only seen a *specimen* of them all, but he had both *seen* and conversed with the *De'il*. His interview with Satan was in the neighbourhood of Lecropt, at a place called Mill-Scive-Bank, when returning that way one evening from Stirling; but the particulars of that interview with the Prince of Darkness the Laird would never divulge, only this much, that it was about some cantrips which had been cast by *Piece-Mornin'*, a Logie witch, which the Laird had discovered, and which had so much displeased the *De'il* that he ventured to attempt terrifying the Laird from using his herbs in removing witch-spells for the future. The Laird knew, indeed, the virtues of many wild-plants, and in his latter days became celebrated from his laudable endeavours to turn his knowledge in this respect into the proper channel, by administering decoctions for the removal of complaints. And let it not be said that such superstitious notions are inconsistent with the character of an honest upright man in those days. It is certainly true that he himself verily believed in the efficacy of his own nostrums in preventing evil spirits from doing mischief to erring mortals, and in averting the *scaith* after the charms had been prepared, and also, that he actually had an angry rencontre with Satan on the subject. Even though this were doubted, it is unquestionably true that the best of men have been known at one time in their lives to tell *one* lie to please their customers. The Laird's "*flicht* through the air" with the fairies of Menstry, as related by himself, is allowed to be only a hallucination of the brain, not by any means unworthy of credit. It is not unworthy of record, even in this short sketch of a character now rare, we may say extinct—a character deeply imbued with the religious enthusiasm of 1733, and its concomitant ignorance and superstition.

The Laird had been at Alloa on a visit to a friend, who accompanied him in the evening so far as Menstry, when, after a parting gill, they separated—the Alloa tailor returning by the way he came, and the Laird by the Brae of Menstry, as the nearest way home. At a green brae, adjacent to the farm-house of Loss, the Laird saw, by the clear moonlight, a vast number of little women in *green-gowns* collecting *wingle-straes*, which they tied in small bunches. The Laird observed them with attention, while he leaned on the beam of a *pleuch*, which by chance was there, with the sock and coulter in the *fur*, as it had just been left by the ploughman not an hour before. When the pigmies had collected about a handful each of the *wingle-straes*, one of them, a bonny little kimmer, stepped a-side to the Laird, and bade him just do with the *pleuch-beam* as he would observe her do with the handful of wingle-straes, and he should have a good supper before he went home. The Laird promised obedience, and accordingly, when he saw the Fairy Queen get astride upon her bunch of *wingle-straes*, he *mounted* his plough-beam. The Queen then waved her wand, crying, "Brechin to the Brithal," and instantly the whole group, Laird and all, having repeated *Brechin to the Brithal*, ascended in the air on coursers fleet as the wind, and white as the driven snow. They soon arrived at Brechin, entered the sumptuous apartments *by the key-holes*, preceded by the Fairy Queen; where, invisible to all the guests, they fared of the very best and savoury viands, and drank of the most delicious and costly wines. Having liberally partaken of everything good at Brechin, the Queen waved her switch and cried out, "Cruinan to the Dance," when presently the whole re-passed the key-holes "like a sough o' wind," and found their coursers below them on the outside, panting for the dance at *Cruinan*. Up again they got, high in the air, and were instantly on the wings of the wind, flying to the dance, but just as they had returned to the spot whence they started the Laird, highly elated with the success of the adventure, could not help exclaiming, "Weel done, Watson's auld Pleuch-beam!" which, unfortunately for the Laird, had the effect of undoing the charm, and leaving him astride on the identical *auld pleuch-beam*, and exactly in the same position he had been previous to the commencement of his *flicht* to Brechin. The pretty green-coated fairies, at the same time, disappeared, leaving the Laird to plod his way homeward in the best manner he could—a task which, with his good supper and wine, he felt no difficulty in accomplishing. It was of no use hinting to the Laird, when he told this story, that the *Menstry gill* with the Alloa tailor might possibly have occasioned his *flicht* to Brechin during a nap on *Watson's auld pleuch-beam*—and that instead of an old plough he had, in all likelihood, ascended on a *gill-stoup*. "Na, na," the Laird would reply to any such as ventured to question the truth of his story—"I couldna be mista'en, and ye ken weel aneuch there's mony ane been carried awa' by the fairies, an' never heard o' mair—forbye Davy Rae's wife o' Tullibody, that was seen ridin' on a clud twenty years after she was stown frae her ain man's side, ae Halloween night when he was sleepin'."

But we shall *shut the book*, having read both sides of the Laird's *leaf*, and merely add that he was the last man of his craft in Dunblane—the last tailor of the old school. He would not tell a lie, nor keep ae *clippin'* to his knowledge—and he never was ashamed of the broad-bonnet, the hodden-grey coat, the long gramashes, and the buckled-shoon, while he lived. Above all, he was one who, till death, indignantly scorned to adopt the then newly invented motto, "A remnant *shall* be saved." Peace to his ashes! we shall never see his like again.

VIII.

BILZY YOUNG.

BILZY YOUNG was one of those chattering, unsettled, work-little, dingy, and gill-drinking mortals, who may be found in almost every town and village about the size of Dunblane. Cities of greater extent have their varieties of the same characters, modified by circumstances and the peculiarities of their gibberish. Bilzy was a spare black-visaged creature, about the middle-size. He was a shot-about weaver to trade, resided in the vicinity of a public house, and where, on account of his peculiar humour, he was invited too frequently, treated to as many gills as he could desire, and where his stories were told with the greatest glee. Bilzy used to pique himself most upon telling wonderful stories. He would engage to tell *the greatest lee* of any man in company, and found always plenty to back him when he took a bet on that score with a stranger. One time an English traveller was treating his customers to a bowl in *the Auld Smith's*, when some of the party mentioning Bilzy's eccentricities, the Englishman desired to see him, confident, he said, he should tell a more improbable and wonderful story than any which Bilzy could invent. Bilzy was in consequence sent for, and soon arrived. The glass went freely round, and Bilzy soon fell in close *confab* with the Englishman. "Ye'll be a merchant, noo?" said Bilzy. "A nailer—a manufacturer of *large* nails, my friend," said the Englishman; "I have this day only arrived here from *the moon*, where I was employed driving one of my nails through that orb, to prevent her from falling asunder." "Indeed!" exclaimed Bilzy, readily, "then ye wad surely see *me*—it was *me* man that stood at the back o' the auld shaird and *rooved* yer nail." "There's a *nailer* for ye, lad," added Bilzy in triumph; and a loud *gaffaw* from the assembled guests announced the *defeat* of the Englishman, which he courteously acknowledged, with a compliment to Bilzy for his ready wit; and the *conversation* was again resumed by the Englishman. "You would hear," he observed, while the company listened, "of the extraordinary cabbage lately reared by a gentleman in Yorkshire, second only to the great tree in the ancient King of Babylon's dream, it was a mile in height, and a league in circumference,—and under the shade of which the whole British army might have found shelter from a hurricane ?" Bilzy said he had not heard of that prodigy, but he could now divine the use the immense *capper* which, during all last summer, had been making at Carron. "It was sae wide," he said, "that the men workin' at the tae side couldna hear the men chappin' at the tither, an' sae *deep*, that when ane o' the men let fa' his hammer aff the lip o't, it took an hour to fa' to the boddom." "Beat again!" exclaimed the Englishman—"your capper shall boil my cabbage"—and he called in liquor until every one present was as drunk as a piper, and Bilzy carried hame in a *hurl-barrow*.

On one occasion Bilzy was likely to be out-Heroded in the marvellous by an old Nimrod, whose exploits, as related by himself, left those of Baron Munchausen in the shade. Bilzy, however, determined to equal him even as a hunter, and related the following in the character of himself:—

He said he knew there were two large hares in a park near by, and he determined to have them both. Arriving at the gate, with his dog, early in the morning, he fixed his large gully-knife in the passage, in such a way as he thought would secure the death of one of the hares, while he knew his dog would be certain to catch the other. Having done this, he sent his dog through the park to start the game, which was speedily done, and the dog in full cry after the two hares direct for the gate. But he said he miscalculated the proper position for erecting his gully betwixt the gate-posts, for one hare passed by one side of it, and the other the other side, while his dog, after running straight against the knife, severing himself exactly in two *perpendicularly*, caught both hares in an adjacent park, the several halves of the dog turning to the right and left of the *gully*, pursuing each its own hare, and killing it.

Bilzy Young died about 1800—"waur to water than *corn*" till the last. He was an amusing pot-companion, a garrulous story-teller, and never in his *element* but in the presence of his drouthy cronies and their *little-stoup*.

Original Poetry.

JACOBITICAL SONG.

[The Compiler cannot positively say that the following verses were never before in print. He has rummaged many repositories of Jacobitical lore, expecting to see the Song in a perfect state, but could not find it. As now given, it was taken down from the singing of a working slater in Perth, in 1822.]

I.

O Charlie maun ye lea yer men,
   Wha in their hearts adore ye,—
When ilka Highlan' hill an' glen
   Rings wi' the drums o' Geordie?
O are ye gaun to France or Spain,
   To lea' Auld Scotland fairly—
An' will ye ne'er come back again,
   To mak us happy—Charlie?

Chorus—Let ilka true Highlan' man,
   Wail his far-scattered Clan,
     For his proud Chieftain's fa'n, fairly;
   Nae mair shall our rocky-glens,
   Ringin' to warlike strains,
     Rouse up yer thousan's-tens, Charlie.

II.

The Highland Clans stuck to the haft,
   An' nearly had restor'd ye;
But now ilk Highland Chief that's left,
   Maun live a slave to Geordie.

O wha will till the muirlan' fiel',
    That pays the labour barely ;
The barren heights will never yield,
    Unless it be for Charlie.
        Let ilka true Highlan' man, &c.

III.

For love o' you your fate I'll share,
    Though tyrants a' abhor ye ;
Nae Gaelic Air can please us mair,
    When a' are slaves to Geordie.
Our summer's short, our hairst is cauld,
    Our winter comes right early ;
An' nae mair now the pibroch bauld,
    Ca's up the Clans for Charlie.
        Let ilka true Highlan' man, &c.

IV.

O wha the tartan plaid wad cast
    For him that wad hae gor'd ye ?
His latest breath gang wi' the blast,
    That winds the drone to Geordie.
O wha wad join the red-coat raw,
    That lo'ed auld Scotland dearly—
O wha his Highlan' dirk would draw,
    Unless it war for Charlie.
        Let ilka true Highlan' man, &c.

V.

O wae be to the sons o' Gaul,
    That didna aid afford ye ;
But left our bravest men to fa',
    An' yield the sway to Geordie.
Their promis'd aid was a' a sham ;
    They've ruined Scotland fairly—
They promis'd, but they never cam',
    To aid the cause o' Charlie.

Chorus—Let ilka true Highlan' man,
 Wail his far-scattered Clan,
  For his proud Chieftain's fa'n fairly ;
 Nae mair shall our rocky-glens,
 Ringin' to warlike strains,
  Rouse up yer thousan's-tens, Charlie.

DUNBLANE WELLS.

I boast no muse whose rapid wing,
Rose from the Heliconian spring,—
  And homely is my strain ;
Unknown to Prince, to Power, and Wealth,
I sing the fount of Joy and Health,
  The Waters of Dunblane.

The fiery-cross has ceased to glance ;
The rust consumes the sword and lance ;
  And o'er the wide domain ;
Soft Peace her standard fair unfurls,
* * * * *

Afar, war's deadly shafts may fly,
And sulph'rous clouds obscure the sky,
  Or shroud the mangled slain.
Yea,—Death may reign in thousand storms,
And dire disease in divers forms—
  That never reach Dunblane.

Then, O, ye shattered Sons of Mars ;
Worn down by toils in troublous wars,
  Deep wounds and piercing pain.
Ah ! why those dim and downcast eyes,
And why those groans and mighty sighs,
  When Health flows at Dunblane.

The cheek once of the roses hue,
And "lips like lilies wet with dew,"
   Though sickly, pale, and wan;
May fan the fading blossom up,
Since Health and Beauty fill the cup
   Of Water at Dunblane.

With erring art, no longer prate,
For CELSUS and old HYPOCRAT.
   Confess their labours vain.
And Galen quits his pots and Mugs,
And shop perfum'd with sick'ning drugs,
   For Water at Dunblane.

The heath puts on her purple bloom,
The braes shine bright with yellow broom;
   And waving on the plain,
The rip'ning corn enrich the view,
And opening gowans sip the dew
   That falls upon Dunblane.

The banks look gay in wild-flowers clad,
Beside the cooling hazel-shade;—
   The birch, the oak, the plane.
In robes of white, the hawthorn tree,
And daisies laughing on the lee,
   Bid welcome to Dunblane.

The birds upon the branches sing,
To HIM who made the water spring—
   The falling dew and rain.
Who gave the sweetness to the breeze,
And said to Nature, Heal and please
   The Stranger in Dunblane.

VERSES:

Written on visiting Sheriff-muir, 16th August, 1832.

I.

O Sheriff-muir, thy heathy dales,
   All in their sheen of purple light,
Divided by the mountain-rills,
   In verdure-fringed compartments bright,
   Now burst on my enraptur'd sight.

II.

My early days dear spot were pass'd,
   With bosom-bounding light in thee,
And all my youthful mind impress'd,
   Recurs to mournful memory,
   While thee in all thy bloom I see.

III.

That burn yet wimples down the howe,
   Where mony a happy day I pass'd;
And there is still the very knowe,
   Where wi' my plaid around me cast,
   I lov'd to brave the summer-blast.

IV.

And here yet stands the lowly cot,
   Where first these eyes beheld the light,
That screen'd me oft in summer hot,
   And 'gainst cauld Winter's stormy spite,
   Me shielded many a drifty night.

V.

These rugged walls—I know each stone—
   That well known mire-thatched roof that bear,
And graven there by him that's gone,
   His name remains—the shepherd here—
   His honour'd name,—my father dear.

VI.

Alas! the hands that rudely traced
   These forms so rustic, artless, wry,
Now moulder in the silent dust—
    While care-beset, and way-worn, I
    Full oft forget I too must die.

VII.

O Sheriff-muir, thy heather-bells,
   Once more relieve my weary e'e,
May I aye love when woe assails,
    To lean me down and dream o' thee,
    And them now gone so dear to me.

VIII.

O then, may aye my slumbers deep,
   Be haunted by thy image fair,
My wakening wish that I could sleep;
    And free from sorrow, free from care,
    Dream o' the past for evermair.

STANZA.

Written on Dunmyot, 30th April, 1834.

From the brow of Dunmyot, steep, rugged, and bare,
   When I view thee thou sweet *Airthrie;*
Thy lawns, woods, and lakes, and thy mansion-house fair,
   I muse on Elysium in thee.
But to know that the shade of SIR RALPH hovers there,
   His guardian attendant to be;
In the CONFLICTS OF PEACE,* as his grandsire in WAR,
   Who is first in the ranks of the Free.
To know that the Youth who inherits that name,
Dare lead us in Union our Rights to reclaim—
My bosom is lit with a holy flame,
   As enraptured I gaze on thee.

* An Election for the County of Perth was on the following day.

THE WIVES O' DUNBLANE.

I.

When gallant young Charlie cam' down to Dunblane,
Ilk wife made him welcome an' his Highlan' men;
The distaff was brandish'd o'er ilk flashin' e'e,
As the wives vow'd to fight, if their husbands should flee,
But the wives o' Dunblane that in ages o' yore,
Felt delight at the glance of the Highland claymore.
Wad now i' their sarks, at its glitterin' sheen,
Run screamin' out "Murder!"—the Wives o' Dunblane.

II.

The Wives o' Dunblane, when Duke William cam' down,
To ransack and plunder their loyal auld town;
Ilk bauld supple carlin her black fulzie-can,
Had ready to pour on the bluidy young man.
But now when the red maun prevail o'er the green—
The scarlet robe flaunt where the tartan was seen;
Ilk light gawky jade, if a sodger she saw,
Would loup frae her mammy, an' wi' him gae awa'.

III.

The auld wives o' Dunblane, wi' the green manky gown,
Were true to their joes an' ne'er on them did frown;
Nor lazy, nor loun-like, was ane o' them seen,
Wi' the muckle-wheel birrin' frae mornin' till een.
But the Wives o' Dunblane, wha for ages before,
Toil'd eydent an' carefu' within their ain door,
Now saunter about or sit on the door-stane,
Each huggin' a baby—the Wives o' Dunblane.

IV.

Auld Wives o' Dunblane—they were trig, they were clean,
Wi' their cloaks an' their sowbacks whare'er they were seen;
Clad in their ain makin' an' spinnin' an' a',
They stour'd to the kirk an' the market fu' bra'.

But Lizzy, an' Lilly, an' Meg o' Dunblane,
Sae thrifty an' healthy, are a' dead an' gane ;
While their gyte taupy dochters in cotton-duds trail,
On their husbands, their bairnies, an' neighbours to rail.

THE BRAES O' CALDHAME.

I.

The Braes o' Caldhame in the ages of yore,
Were a cold sloping dale, and a wild barren moor ;
But now they are shelter'd and cultur'd sae braw—
The gloom o' Caldhame is for ever awa'.

II.

By the Braes o' Caldhame is a field o' the slain,
Around its memorial the grey "Stan'in Stane,"
Which Wallace, the mighty, with spear and with bow,
Had bath'd in the blood o' the Suthron foe.

III.

The Braes o' Caldhame, they were bleak, they were brown,
When the Highland claymore in "the Shirra-moor" shone ;
But now they are green—wi' the lamb on the lea,
The ox in the park, and the bird in the tree.

IV.

Ye clear mountain springlets that ripple so cold,
How fondly my heart beats when you I behold ;
A school-boy, ye springlets, your mazes I trac'd—
By your margins the wild-bee and butterfly chac'd.

V.

Thou wild-dashing Wharrie, that foams through Glentye,
O how starts the tear-drop when thee I descry ;
A thousand times, Wharrie, I've play'd by thy stream,
Or trouted thy linns wi' the Youth o' Caldhame.

VI.

Through dark disappointment, and sorrow, and woe,
Since I left these sweet scenes, I've been destined to go;
Yet the glooms of misfortune disperse like a dream,
From " the mounds of the dead, when I see thee, Caldhame.

NOTES.

The "Caldhame" alluded to in the above verses (for there are many places in the country which are known by the same appellation), is the name of a compact, isolated, and now fertile portion of high ground, comprising upwards of 250 acres, situated in Sheriffmuir, now the property, by lineal inheritance, of a gentleman in Perth. From a bleak and barren hill-side, this farm within the last sixty years has become, by mere dint of culture, what has not inaptly been termed an *oasis* in a Libyan desert. Viewed from the battle-ground of Sheriff-muir, it affords a fine resting-place to the eye, after traversing the wide and withering district by which it is environed. Divided and subdivided as Caldhame is, by a series of thriving plantations with its elegant mansion-house piercing amidst a clump of trees on the brow of the hill—its green enclosures on which the cattle are browsing in perfect shelter—a beholder from the *scene* above-mentioned, cannot but feel pleasure and delight to witness such a specimen of agricultural improvement, where all before was marsh and heath, and where a circumambient and extensive waste still continues to represent its primitive condition.

STANZA II.

Blind Harry says an army of 10,000 English were killed to a man in Sheriff-muir, by the immortal Wallace, with 8000 Scots. This is corroborated by tradition, yet current in the district, which points out the "field of the slain," about a mile to the north-east of Caldhame, in the centre of which the "Stan'in Stane" yet remains as a monument of the victory.

STANZA VI.

The graves, or rather trenches, where the dead were buried on the battle-field of Sheriff-muir, are yet readily distinguished. This wellknown action, fought 12th November, 1715, it may be added, is yet referred to as an epoch by old people resident in the district, as "that year the Highlandmen ran." It would appear that those brave fellows, the Highlanders, previous to that day, were deemed invincible by their Lowland neighbours, and incapable of flying from their enemies.

DONAL' O' DUNBLANE.

When Donal' left his native glen,
    An' clear Loch-Earn side ;
The bonniest lassies o' Dunblane
    Strave wha wad be his bride.
They'd left their dads and mammie's dear—
    Their friends an' kindred a',
An' buckled up their hammell'd gear,
    An' wi' him run awa'.

Chorus—But Donal' leukit aye sae hie,
    Sae far aboon them a' ;
    He thocht an' thocht he'd wait awee,
    Till better wad befa'.

Young Jeannie kemb'd her raven hair,
    An' lang she buskit braw—
An' lang at every kirk and fair,
    She bore the gree awa'.
An' mony a proffer'd heart and hand,
    Her love-lorn bosom knew ;
Tho' stealin' owre her a' she fand,
    Her love for Donal' grew.

    But Donal' leukit aye sae hie, &c.

An' Lizzy laced her genty waist,
    Sae jimpy neat an' sma' ;
An' wow, but she gaed featly dress'd,
    To steal his heart awa'.
Her mam bade Donal' to his tea,
    Her grandeur a' to shaw ;
An' tell'd what riches Liz wad hae,
    An' wha might get them a'.

    But Donal' leukit aye sae hie, &c.

Blythe Jessy wi' the poutin' mou',
  An' lovely laughing e'e;
Tho' ane sought a' the kintra through,
  Her match he wadna see.
Quo' she the lad's owre blate to woo,
  He surely wad hae me;
An' this is Hogmanay I trow,
  I'll gang awa' an' see.

  But Donal' leukit aye sae hie, &c.

But time and tide nae man may bide,
  An' beauty fades awa';
Young Jeannie is anither's bride—
  An' Lizzy's woo'd an' a'.
Blythe Jessy's at her ain fire-side,
  Wi' todlin bairnies twa—
While Donal' wi' a grow-grey head,
  His ain cauld coal maun blaw.

  For Donal' leukit aye sae hie, &c.

Now Donald when ye're turning auld,
  And ken ye war mista'en;
An' trum'lin' a' in winter cauld,
  When ye lie down yer lane—
Amang the blankets mony a fauld,
  To mourn the day that's gane;
Ye maun na hear and think to scald,
  The lasses o' Dunblane.

  For ye aye leukit up sae hie,
   Sae far aboon them a'—
  Ye thocht an' thocht ye'd wait awee,
   Till better wad befa'.

TO THE WILLOW.—1823.

I.

Hang thy head, thou hoary Willow ;
   None but thou congenial art—
Mournful plant! be by my pillow,
   Droop thee o'er this dying heart.
The threads of vital life are breaking,
The golden seat of mind is aching ;
The glimmering beams of joy dividing,
Grow dim in twilight shades receding.

II.

While life's last pulse beat wildly fluttering,
   Still must I doat on scenes of old ;
And, when estrayed, weak reason muttering,
   Must with her raving converse hold.
And oh! when mind runs thus estrang'd,
Sure, then she'll doubt not my regard ;
When this sad heart at life's last eve,
Her—her alone regrets to leave.

III.

Mournful plant! wave o'er this bosom,
   Sad drooping shrub my laurel be ;
Grey are thy leaves, dull is thy blossom,
   Unlike the dream that guided me.
Yet, hail! O fate, dull emblem dreary,—
Wave o'er this heart and I will wear thee ;
And when I'm gone—for her I mourn,
Thou'lt drop clear dew-drops on my urn.

MOONY MADNESS.

In full refulgence o'er the broom-clad braes, (1)
The Moon diffus'd her paley-yellow rays;
While on the height in selfish-frown elate,
The "self-taught genius" ruminating sat.
Huge ancient volumes circumscribed his shade, (2)
Large rolls of parchment round him were displayed;
Oft rose his head, as if his heart assay'd
To pour its feelings in the ambient void—
And seem'd invoking every power in vain;
Thoughts uncondens'd long lagging on his brain.
While, with clench'd fangs, he smote his every side,
While his stretch'd jaws yawn'd horrible and wide.
While, light'ning like the foliage green he tore—
Or bulls incens'd the thorny furze that gore.
Long did th' incessant epileptic throw,
Rebound his heaving carcase to and fro;
While grass, and earth, and shrub around he strew'd,
And his own blood, his earthy hands imbued—
Even till the efforts of his burning soul,
Burst every chain of bodily control.

Like some slow earthquake or a groaning bear,
Writhing beneath the hunter's murdering spear;
Now hideous growlings from his dank trunk rung,
In stammering belched o'er his frothy tongue—
Till maddening thought in broken words gave way,
The violent engine of his heart to sway;
And "oratorial" through his strain'd jaws burst, (3)
Vociferations,—horrible,—accurs'd.

"What!" said the frantic man (like priesthood blown—
Confronting heaven) wild pointing at the moon;
"Am I—a man of knowledge and of worth,
"Theologist, and glory of the earth!" (4)

(Here, starting to his feet, he struck his breast,
Like tortur'd ghost of murderer deceas'd.)
" Must I be thus abus'd ?—the slanderer's tale !
" The laugh of guilt ! the butt of ridicule !
" Am I—a man with every talent blest—
" The censor'd reptile of ludicrous jest ?
" To thee, pale Orb ! I ' *orally* ' appeal ; (5)
" Thou oft in *full* hast heard my midnight wail.
" Oh ! from thy influence in baleful gleam,
" Wither their germins dread and blast their fame ;
" Their machinations on their heads recoil,
" In dark oblivion hush their every toil.
" What ! though in secret glowing love may err,
" And nights of lust succeed long hours of prayer ;
" Must I—whose conduct otherwise is just,
" Ingloriously, for that, be thus traduc'd ?
" Thou shining Moon !—ye twinklers of the night,
"Confound ! curse !—seize them, and their prospects blight !"
So did the M———ejonian trump address (6)
The silver source of his insane distress ;
Then rais'd his hat to wipe his smoking hair,
And show his eye-balls' red terrific glare.
While bending low before his goddess bright,
A thousand times he bade the Moon good night.

NOTES.

(1) In the neighbourhood of a beautiful sheet of water, much frequented in winter by the " Dunblane Curling Club," are these *braes*. Our hero frequently may be seen, when the moon " shines broad and bright," traversing here at midnight.

(2) In his nocturnal rambles he invariably carries weight—Latin, French, and even huge Hebrew volumes constitute this, although he is entirely ignorant of any of these languages. He often solves a number of geometrical problems by moonlight, and, therefore, necessarily, must have his figures and instruments.

(3) " Oratorial." A technical word of his own, here used with much propriety.

(4) He requested his friends and correspondents to address to him " Theologist of the Academy School."

WOMAN.

Of all the dreary ills that cross us,
Weary mortals lingering here;
Darling Woman most perplexes—
Nought but she can really vex us,
  Who can slighting Woman bear?

Long I lov'd, and lov'd with honour,
Ere that love I did declare;
Would to Heaven I'd never known her—
Never—never—never seen her—
  Slighting Woman who can bear?

Why to double scorning treat him—
Him that pines in virtuous love;
Why refuse one time to meet him,
Where the very night-birds hoot him,
  Lonely in the shady grove?

O Woman thou art deem'd a blessing;
Why to that must I be blind—
·Thou art sometimes worth possessing,
But even then, oh! how distressing,
  Thou art fickle as the wind.

WISPY.

—— Lashing blasts drave heavy on,
—— Howling winds did sighing moan,
An' no a single starnie shone,
    To cheer the night;
When Davy wander'd lang alone,
    A weary wight.

---

(5) Another word (orally) peculiarly applied by our genius.—See *Stirling Journal*, 3d January, 18—.
(6) "M——ejonian." His Ethical system is quite original—which it will be necessary to distinguish, as he has a number of disciples. I have termed it after his own name—surely with no impropriety.

His maukins o'er his shouthers strung—
His wild-fowl at his shot-bag slung,
His *Spunk*-flask at his hurdies hung.
    Benighted soul!
His *Spunkie*-piece his only rung,
    To point a hole!

Headlong he over hillocks rush'd,
And wet through bogs and mosses smash'd,
He glower'd—he gaed—he paus'd—he dash'd,
    His theme a ghaist!
When blink!—a light—his fears were hush'd,
    To be increas'd.

The glimmering beam began to dance,
An' through his brains confus'd to glance,
Then sportively it shot askance,
    Just at his nose!
He wallop'd o'er wi' heavy wince,
    An' boked brose.

How lang he lay he could not tell;
When he cam hame he kens himsel;—
He's sure some bogle het frae hell,
    Did at him grasp;
But a' around impute the spell
    To "Will o' Wisp."

FRAGMENT.

Dark lower'd the night, and o'er the plains,
The raving winds and dashing rains,
    Had storm'd the winter day;
And matted clouds a dismal shade—
The evening's thickening veil had spread,
    While wandering I did stray.

. . . .

And does (thought I), this cloud of death,—
Those pallid sparks from hell beneath,
      Predict approaching fate;
Propitious to a dread design,
The horrors of the night combine—
      And I'm bewilder'd late.

. . . . . .

By lambent lamp that pale appear'd,
A spectre ghast himself uprear'd,
      And fix'd my wondering gaze.
Around him hung a tartan plaid—
A tartan bonnet on his head,
      Envelop'd in a blaze.

. . . . . .

THE DUNBLANE WIFE'S LILT.

There was an auld wife—she had nae bairns,
An' she teuk the Pint-stoup into her arms;
An' aye she sang—" Balillilly-loo,
May ye ne'er be toom till I be *fou*."

NOTES TO THE BIOGRAPHICAL SKETCHES.

No. I.—It cannot be said that "Bessy Stein" is now *alive*,—such a personage having been conjured up to embody facts and circumstances which must have been observed by every thinking mortal who knows human nature, and who has resided in this neighbourhood within the last *forty* years.

No. III.—No fictitious character was "Henry Reid;"—and the facts here recorded, and the *shades* given to the character, may be considered just.

No. IV.—This article must be allowed to be *hyperbolical*—nay, fictitious, as no such individual as "The Muckle Wife o' Bithergirse" ever existed in Bithergirse. But let the inhabitants residing within a wide part of a bleak and barren district north of Dunblane ask themselves whether all the circumstances here recorded have not happened within their bounds and *elsewhere* " in their day."

No. V.—This was a *Genuine* of the old school—before the introduction of "Jonathan's Abstinence *Merchandise*,"—when "every honest man had a *right* to do with *his ain* what he liket."

No. VI.- -Another true CHUCK of the primitive times, when the smoke escaped from the domiciles of our ancestors in *horizontal* volumes, in preference to the new mode of issuing perpendicularly.

No. VII.—The last of THE Tailors.

SUBSCRIBERS

TO

Monteath's Dunblane Traditions.

DUNBLANE.

	Copies.
Sheriff Colquhoun,	5
Rev. A. Henderson,	2
Dr. Stewart,	3
Thomas Bayne, Feus,	1
James Monteath, merchant,	1
William Fogo, baker,	1
William Kinnaird, tailor,	1
William M'Kenzie, smith,	1
Robert Sharp, flesher,	1
A. Morrison, weaver, Bridge-end,	1
John Guthrie, wright, do.,	1
John Scobie, weaver, do.,	1
James Sharp, agent,	1
Peter Bennet, weaver, Bridge-end,	1
James Lewis Eadie, do.	1
James Anderson, weaver, do.	1
James Reid, Ramoyle,	1
William Paterson, weaver, Feus,	1
John Kinross, baker,	1
Andrew Mallach, Esq.,	1
R. M'Donald, weaver,	1
John Robertson, Ramoyle,	1
James Spudie, weaver, do.	1
William Jack, do., do.	1

	Copies.
James Mitchell, weaver, Ramoyle,	1
Henry Meiklejohn do	1
James Wilson, spirit-dealer,	1
Walter Kinross, meal-monger,	1
James Lennox, weaver, Ramoyle,	1
James Bryce, do., do.,	1
William King, do., do.,	1
John Graham, merchant,	1
Dr. Douglas,	1
John Bayne, weaver, Feus,	1
David Crawford, do., do.	1
Peter Roy, do., do.	1
James Ritchie, do., do.	1
John Stewart, do., do.	1
James Dawson, Feus,	1
John Hutchison, do.	1
John Jack, weaver, do.	1
Thomas M'Ewen, shoemaker, do.	1
David Clow, weaver, Bridge-end,	1
James Eason, do., do.	1
George Christie, writer,	1
Peter Bayne, flesher,	1
John Malcolm, Kirk-street,	1
W. Stewart, Brae-port,	1
Alexander Dow, Ramoyle,	1
Hugh Cameron, do.,	1
John Sorley, do.,	1
John M'Lachlan, nailor,	1
Thomas Barty, Esq.,	2
Peter M'Kenzie, writer,	1
Alexander Dow, shoemaker,	1
R. Stewart, Mill-row,	1
W. Meiklejohn, do.,	1
Henry Eadie, weaver, do.,	1
John Malloch, do.,	1
William Scobie, weaver, do.,	1
Thomas M'Ewan, do., do.,	1
James Anderson, do., do.,	1
John Cameron, shoemaker,	1
John Reid, writer,	1
John Campbell, teacher,	1
W. Stirling, Esq., architect,	4
D. Stewart, teacher,	1

	Copies.
Donald Martin, weaver, Feus,	1
James Brown, do., Mill-row,	1
Archd. Paterson, do., do.,	1
John M'Gruthar, Esq.,	3
William Lucas, flesher,	2
Duncan M'Laren, High-street,	1
Thomas Gow, grocer,	2
Charles Meiklejohn,	2
William Walker, writer,	1
J. S. Thomson, weaver,	1
George Blair, Kippenross,	1
William Tait, Ramoyle,	1
James King, elder,	1
John Lennox, weaver,	1
Alexander Clark,	1
Peter Whitehead, mason,	1
William Robin, wright,	1
William Hay, weaver,	1
James M'Ewen, clerk,	1
Robert Walker, senior,	3
Thomas M'Ewen, wool-spinner,	1
David Miller, do.	1
John M'Kenzie, wright,	1
James Johnston, smith,	1
Samuel Cameron, wool-spinner,	1
Robert Walker, junior,	2
A. Watson, wool-spinner,	1
Daniel Sillars, do.	1
Thomas Wilson, do.	1
John Grey, carpet-weaver,	1
James Drummond, gamekeeper,	1
R. Bizzet, pensioner,	1
James Forrester, Mill-row,	1
William M'Ewan, Bridge-end,	1
John Frue, writer,	1
Alexander Martin, weaver,	1
William Robertson, junior,	1
William Jack, weaver Ramoyle,	1
John Rattray, do., Bridge-end,	1
Donald Gow, Ramoyle,	1
W. M'Leish, wool-spinner,	1
W. Drysdale, wool-spinner,	1
Thomas Dawson, Barbush,	1

Copies

James Cramb,	1
John Leishman,	1
Robert Morrison, agent,	1
Alexander M'Gregor, Dalhanzie,	1
Walter M'Gregor, Bridge-end,	1
William M'Gregor, teacher,	1
William Christie, Ramoyle,	1
Robert Roy, High Street,	1
W. Meiklejohn, Bridge-end,	1
John Gentle, saddler,	1
William Nicolson, Bridge-end,	1
D. Cameron, slater,	1
Robert Crawford, Barbush,	1
John M'Nie, servant, do.,	1
John Reid, Ochenley,	1
Robert Finlayson, wright, Balhaldie,	1
Duncan Campbell,	1
J. Whitehead, farmer, Corscaple,	1

DOUNE, DEANSTON, &c.

James Smith, Esq.,	2
Alexander Beattie,	2
James Johnston, teacher,	2
William Sharp, mason,	3
Mr. M'Farlane, architect,	3
John Frazer, surgeon,	1
Robert Crawford, Deanston,	1
John M'Farlane, Doune,	1
Archd. Maxwell, Deanston,	1
Margaret M'Kinlay, do.,	1
Alexander Stewart, do.,	1
Robert Congalton, do.,	1
Andrew Fleming, do.,	1
James M'Dall, do.,	1
John Mitchell, do.,	1
John Crawford, do.,	1
Robert Dawson, do.,	1
William M'Allister, do.,	1
Adam Weire, do.,	1
William Monteath, do.,	1
James Omar, do.,	1
Matthew M'Kay, do.,	1

Andrew Meiklejohn, Deanston,
W. Gordon Lennox, do., ...
Peter M'Queen, do., ...
James Armstrong, do., ...
James Carlin, do., ...
Alexander M'Farlane, do., ...
John M'Lean, Doune, ...
A. Jamieson, surgeon, ..
William Bain, shoemaker, ...
Peter Burns, wright, ...
David Dewar, clock-maker, ...
William Bayne, shopkeeper, ...
Edward Bayne, clothier, ...
Robert Miller. innkeeper, ...
James Bain, Bridge-of-Teith, ...
John Gillespie, Deanston, ...
Christian M'Laren, do., ...
James Stewart, do., ..
Anne M'Laren, do., ...
Alexander Halbert, do., ...
Janet Carmichael, do., ...
John Robertson, do., ...
Aaron Hastie, do., ...
W. Congalton, do., ...
James Scobie, do., ...
James Irvine, do., ...
John M'Craw, do., ...
John M'Laren, do., ...
Joseph Ronald, do., ...
John M'Gregor, do., ...
Peter Anderson, do., ..
George Sharp, do., ...
Robert Winton, do., ...
W. Faichney, do., ..
John M'Donald, do., ...
John Martin, do., ...
James Gillespie, do., ...
James M'Nab, do., ..
George Sneddon, do., ...
James Fisher, do., ...
W. Balfour, slater, Doune, ...
John M'Kinlay, farmer, ...
William M'Arthur, farmer, ...

130

                   Copies

James Roy, gardener, Clangregor,	1
Robert Ferguson, smith, do.,	1
John Cairns, farmer,	1
Thomas Paterson, ploughman,	1
John Miller, farmer,	1
James M'Arthur, farmer,	1
W. Blacklock, Callander,	1
Duncan M'Pherson, do,,	1
A. Buchanan, shoemaker, do.,	1
Robert M'Laren, hosier, do.,	1
A. Ferguson, shoemaker,	1
Finlay Ferguson, do.,	1
Donald Ferguson, do.,	1
Peter M'Beath, merchant,	1
Donald M'Innes, tailor,	1
R. M'Nabb, mason,	1
James Taylor, watchmaker,	1
A. M'Grigor, innkeeper, Callander,	1
Donald M'Farlane, shoemaker,	1
Duncan M'Kinlay, Wester Watcher,	1
Peter M'Leish, sawyer	1
George Manwell, shoemaker,	1
Donald M'Laren, tailor,	1
Angus M'Donald, shoemaker,	1
—— Malcolm, merchant,	1
Walter Henderson, smith, Anchlistir,	1
Walter Balfour, slater, Doune,	1
George Bryce, smith,	1
Thomas Stewart, tailor,	1
John Rennie, toll-bar, Dallin,	1
Peter M'Laren, mason, near Thornhill,	1
Andrew M'Laren, tailor, Deanston,	1
Janet M'Donald, do.,	1
John Brown, slater, Doune,	1
Charles M'Nie, mason, Drumoagh,	1
John M'Culloch, tailor, Thornhill,	1
John M'Gregor, merchant,	1
John Shirra, farmer, Boquhapple,	1
William Thomson, do., Drummore,	1
John Leitch, do.,	1
James Drummond, wright, Doune,	1
James Watt, farmer, Boquhapple,	1
J. M'Culloch, tailor, Thornhill,	1

	Copies
A. Morrison, mason, Norrieston,	1
J. Miller, Middle-Frew,	1
William Forrester,	1
John Dochart, Easter M., Frew.	1
John Paterson, farmer, Moss-side,	1
David Hood, smith, Norrieston,	1
John Stirling, farmer, Boquhapple,	1

STRATHALLAN DISTRICT.

A. Monteath, Greenloaning,	1
Mrs. A. Mitchell, of Glasgow,	1
D. Stoddart, Greenloaning,	1
James Gordon, do.,	1
George Stewart, smith, do.,	1
David Thomson, smith, Ardoch,	1
Robert Kemp, ploughman, Haughs,	1
Denis O'Brien, tailor, Ardoch,	1
John Scott, Allan-bank,	1
William Ferguson, Ardoch,	1
A. M'Gregor, teacher, do.,	1
—— Carmichael, Haugh,	1
James Campbell, gardener, Ardoch,	1
John Morrison, forester, do.	1
Mary Reid, do.	1
Mrs. Jack, vintner, do.,	1
Alexander Jack do.,	1
Peter Clow, miller, Feddal,	1
John M'Ewan, Cambushenie,	1
James Stirling, Craighead,	1
Robert Stirling, Tominoe,	1
M. Finlayson, Shepherd,	1
William Brydie, Beatuck,	1
William M'Innes, farmer,	1
Peter M'Ildowie, do.	1
John Branison,	1
Hugh Dick, Whistle-brae,	1
Lewis Kinross, Loig,	1
Angus Crawford, do.,	1
John Miller, Greenloaning,	1
Peter Comrie, teacher, Balhaldie,	1
James Roy, Balhaldie Inn,	1

John Martin, wright. Balhaldie, ...
James Reid. Nether Cambushinie, ...
James M'Nab, smith, Kinbuck, ...
Robert Clow, farmer, Balhaldie, ...
James Ritchie, Lime-side, ...
Robert Smith, roadman, Rottearns, ...
John M'Nab, smith, do., ...

CRIEFF.

George M'Culloch, teacher, ...
P. Fenwick, watch-maker, ...
—— M'Ewen, do.. ... ...
Thomas M'Donald, teacher, ...
John Kidd, ...
William Clement, grocer, ...
John Miller, grocer, ...
M'Donald & Sons, ...
A. Morris, miller, ...
David Jack, Esq., Dalvreck-mills, ...
J. Dougal, surgeon, Muthill, ...

BLACKFORD.

William Fletcher, ...
John Stalker, manufacturing agent,
James Scobie, weaver, ...
James Marshall, do. ... ...
Daniel M'Laurin, ...
Peter Caw, ...
James Smeaton, ...
W. Monteath, Caldhame, ...
John Davidson, ...
William Davidson, ...
James Gloag, junr., ...
Robert Crichton, ...
William Lockhart, ...
Hugh Gordon, ...
Robert Brown, ...
Thomas Martin, precentor, Alloa, ...

STIRLING, &c.

Lord Abercromby,
James Lucas, Esq.
F. W. Clarke, Esq.,
John Sawers, Esq.
William Galbraith, Esq.,
George M'Gowan, Esq.,
James Monteath, Esq.,
Alexander Boyd, Esq.,
Ebenezer Gentleman, Esq.,
James Mathie, Esq.,
Andrew Crawford, Esq.,
James Kerr, Esq.,
William Mackison,
John Ferguson,
Duncan M'Nab,
Andrew M'Millan,
Michael Laing, hair-dresser,
Banks Somerville,
John Maxwell, banker, ...
William Whitehead, Castle,
Rev. Mr. M'Lauchlane, ...
Patrick G. Morrison,
William H. Forrest, surgeon,
John Dick, manufacturer,
John Hamilton, tailor, ...
Miss Taylor, ...
James Drummond, merchant,
William Hutton, writer,
Adam Steel, junior, merchant,
B. Williams, ...
Robert Steel, candle-maker,
John Frazer, teacher, ...
James Reid, York Place,
A. M'Martin, Custom-house,
William Marshall, agent, Cowan-street,
John Finlayson, spirit-dealer, do.
Malcolm Lennox, weaver,
John Watson, spirit-dealer,
J. Alexander, ...
David M'Farlane, spirit-dealer,
John M'Farlane, pensioner,

	Copies.
James Finlayson, sen., slater,	1
John Ramsay, gardener,	1
John Goodall, painter,	1
Robert Downie, cooper,	1
William Nicol,	1
J. Campbell, spirit-dealer,	1
William Macaree,	1
Thomas Gillies, ironmonger,	1
A. Telford, oil and colour-man,	1
David Turnbull, smith,	1
Robert Moffat, Cowan-street,	1
Robert Millar, writer,	1
David Gillespie, Cowan-street,	1
Andrew Buchanan, grocer,	1
—— Stevenson, Bridge,	1
John M'Rorie, Cowan-street	1
—— Thomson, do.	1
John Finlayson, manufacturer,	1
Robert Crawford, grocer,	1
John Murray, Esq. of Livilands,	6
J. Rollo, merchant, Bannockburn,	1
John Mowat, foreman, do.	1
Thomas Gray, baker, do.	1
Peter M'Naughton, do.	1
James Robertson, schoolmaster, do.	1
John Wilson. Esq., do.	1
David Eadie, weaver, do.	1
John Glass, do. do.	1
James Stewart, do. do.	1
Dr Buchanan, do.	1
Robert Horley, do.	1
William Paterson, clerk, do.	1
J. Murdoch, carpet-weaver, do.	1
James Mitchell, do., do.	1
Peter Murdoch, do.	1
John Watson, do.	1
James Ritchie, do.	1
John Paterson, do.	1
James Graham, do.	1
James Thomson, do.	1
John Turnbull, Milton,	1
James Ferries, Whins,	1
John Campbell, Cambusbarron,	1

	Copies.
James Gray, Bearside, ...	1
Dr. Rutherford, Bridge-of-Allan,	2
Peter Dochart, teacher, do.	1
Andrew Kinross, weaver, do.	1
C. N. Rutherford, do.	1
Robert Baird, do.	1

www.ingramcontent.com/pod-product-compliance
Lightning Source LLC
Chambersburg PA
CBHW031503160426
43195CB00010BB/1097